TEACHING MATHEMATICS FOR FIRST AND SECOND GRADES IN WALDORF SCHOOLS

Math curriculum, basic concepts, and their developmental foundation

by

Ernst Schuberth

RUDOLF STEINER COLLEGE PRESS
9200 Fair Oaks Boulevard · Fair Oaks, California

This book appeared in German under the title, *Der Anfangsunterricht in der Mathematik an Waldorfschulen,* published in 1993 by Verlag Freies Geistesleben, Stuttgart.
ISBN 3-7725-0263-6

Translation by Kim Holscher, Seattle, Washington; with editorial attention by Astrid Schmitt-Stegmann, Fair Oaks, California.
Other translations are available in Russian, Japanese, and Rumanian.

ISBN 0 - 945803 - 37 - 0

Rudolf Steiner College Press
9200 Fair Oaks Boulevard
Fair Oaks, California 95628

TABLE OF CONTENTS

PREFACE

For Waldorf teachers, math is often one of the more difficult subjects to teach. On the one hand, memories of our own school days can cloud our view of the developmental needs of the child, while on the other hand, Steiner's many indications do not form a cohesive structure for the math curriculum. Thus, many different ways of teaching were developed during Waldorf pedagogy's seventy-year history. This diversity underscores the responsibility each teacher carries for his/her lessons.

This guide does not intend in any way to diminish this responsibility, but seeks to contribute to a unified view of Steiner indications for a developmentally appropriate math curriculum.

Our approach may differ from existing ones, mainly in directly and quickly beginning math activities and avoiding pictures when introducing the numbers. Other differences may exist as well.

These pages contain my own experiences as well as those of colleagues who learned this method in workshops and applied it in their own teaching. I would like to express my gratitude to all those who contributed.

It is hoped that the following description does not lead to dogmatic fixation on these methods. The author would appreciate critical comments, new perspectives on human development, and relevant additions of all kinds.

Ernst Schuberth
Mannheim, Pentecost 1992

PREFACE TO THE ENGLISH LANGUAGE EDITION

Soon after the completion of the German text, Kim Holscher of Seattle undertook the task of translating it into English. She approached this work with a creativity that makes it easier for an American to read. Readers of both languages will be able to remark the differences that have been introduced for improved clarity. I wish to express here my deep thanks to Ms. Holscher for her contribution.

Since the appearance of the German edition (Stuttgart 1993) translations have appeared in English, Russian, Japanese, and Rumanian. Many positive reactions have confirmed that the path suggested here can be fruitfully followed. In particular the positive comments of colleagues in traditional public schools were a confirmation that Waldorf pedagogy can be generally applied wherever children are instructed. It is not only fruitful for children in Waldorf schools.

I am well aware how much in this small book can and should be elaborated. Nevertheless this second edition, published in America, contains only minimal corrections. The brevity leaves to the reader the freedom to pursue a fully individual path with his/her class and the reports of colleagues show what varied paths are possible.

Some readers have found the chapter on math weaknesses to be especially interesting. Particularly here, further research should be pursued but under current circumstances it has not been possible to carry it on.

Ernst Schuberth
Rudolf Steiner College, Fair Oaks, California, Summer 1997

THE FIRST MATH BLOCK

While preparing to teach the first math block, we think back to the very first day of school. We talked with the children about the reasons they attend school. We made them aware of the variety of skills adults possess that they themselves have not yet achieved, such as reading, writing, calculating, making and reading maps, speaking foreign languages, and many more abilities that life requires. Immediately after this conversation we taught the children the basic forms of the straight and the curved line. (See Rudolf Steiner, *Practical Advice for Teachers.*)

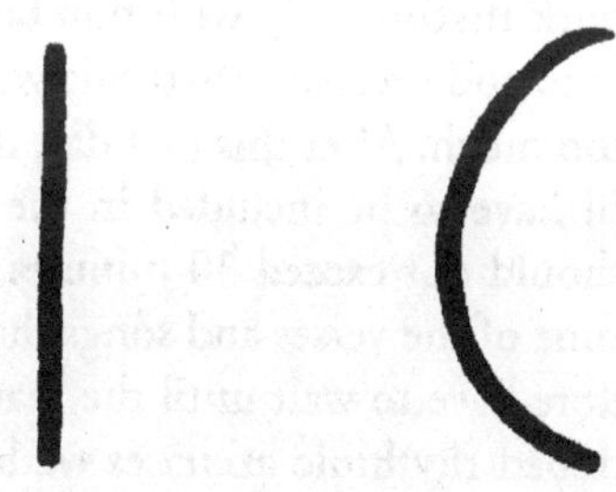

figure 1

From this lesson we developed the first Form Drawing block, which trains the children's sense of form, increases hand flexibility, and therefore prepares the child for writing.

During the second block we introduced the first letters. By developing the consonants out of pictures, we enable the children to relate to their attributes and forms. The letters remain alive because they emerge like skeletal abstractions from natural shapes. These two blocks led us into fall, and they now can be followed by the first math block.

This chapter describes a hypothetical lesson plan that highlights the essential structural elements. Each teacher will have to adapt this proposal to his/her own teaching style and group of children. This example is meant to show one possible application of the general principles.

The First Math Lesson

At the start of the new block something slightly different and new can now replace the usual morning rituals.

Our first suggestion is to reduce the rhythmic exercises (morning circle activities) of the main lesson to the barest minimum for this first day of the new block: the greeting, morning verse, and a few familiar items. This is recommended because we will work rhythmically with numbers in the learning part of today's lesson, and excessive rhythmic work would "loosen up" the children too much. After this first day, the rhythmic work with numbers will have to be included in the regular rhythmic exercises, which should not exceed 30 minutes or the lesson will be unbalanced. Some of the verses and songs that the children are used to will therefore have to wait until the math block is over.

After the shortened rhythmic exercises we let the children sit down and refer again—just as at the beginning of the first writing block—to the conversation of the first day of school. We could say, for example: *You have been in school for quite some time now. You have learned how to draw forms and even letters and your hands are very skillful now. And now we want to begin to learn something that adults have to be able to do very well in their life. Just think about your parents and about all the things they have to consider for your family's needs. I'm sure you know that your parents earn money to live on and that with this money they buy things such as bread, shoes, clothes, even cars and many other things. But we can't buy everything that we want—you surely have noticed that your parents won't buy you everything that you want. They don't buy everything they want either! This is very important because they have to think first about what your family needs. Do you know what some of the things are that your parents have to pay for?*

The children will be able to name many items ranging from food and clothes to rent, heat, electricity, and water. We could then continue with: *You see how many things your parents have to think about if they want to be good fathers and mothers. They have to be able to divide up the money so that they can pay for all those necessities. Somebody who is able to divide up money well is good at calculating, and there is an important secret to this: if you can calculate well, you will always have something left over to share with your friends or with needy people. And this important skill of calculating we now want to learn so that you will all become capable people.*

With this introductory discussion (which should not be too long) we touch on a theme that is crucial to holistic math teaching: proceeding from the whole—in this case the parents' income—we divide or structure it into its parts. This is illustrated in figure 2, as opposed to the process of additive enlarging, which is shown in figure 3.

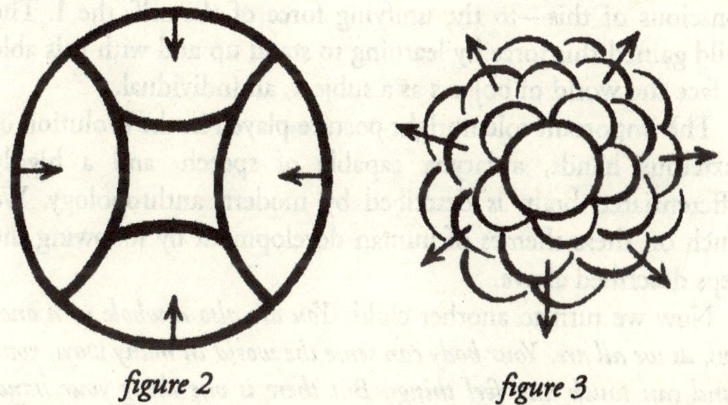

figure 2 *figure 3*

The first process is an inner differentiation, the second an additive enlarging. This contrast is discussed further in the section on analytical and synthetic thinking, see pp. 30-31.

figure 4

After this conversation with the children we reach for the rotten stick we brought with us (following an indication Steiner gave in his lectures in Torquay, *The Kingdom of Childhood*), break it and say: *See, I can break the stick into two sticks. But I cannot break you into two people, Monica, because you are a whole, a oneness. I will use this sign for one.*

Here, the straight line from the first school day reappears with a new meaning. Where then it represented the upright posture the child achieved at age one, it now points—the child is not conscious of this—to the unifying force of the self, the I. The child gained this force by learning to stand up and with it is able to face the world of objects as a subject, an individual.

The important role upright posture played in the evolution of dexterous hands, a larynx capable of speech, and a highly differentiated brain is described by modern anthropology. We touch on these themes of human development by following the steps described above.

Now we turn to another child: *You are also a whole or a oneness, as we all are. Your body can sense the world in many ways, your hand can touch and feel things. But there is one thing your hand cannot feel.* Generally the children will find out that the hand cannot feel itself. It is like other organs of perception: the healthy eye does not see itself; the ear does not hear itself. Thus, the hand that touches something feels the object it touches, not primarily itself.

Your hand cannot feel itself, then. But you have two hands and they can touch each other. They are a twosome, and for that we will make this sign:

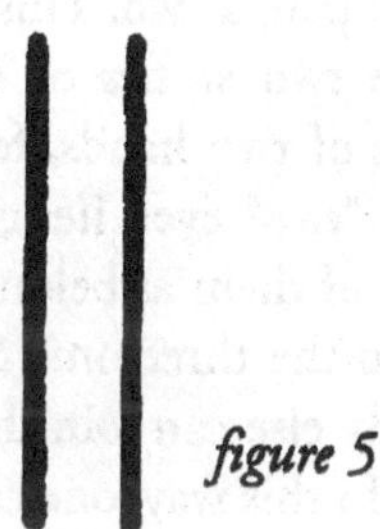

figure 5

Again we have mentioned an important theme in human development: the pairing of several human organs and their interplay is a requirement for a healthy childhood. Bilaterally developed organs—eyes, hands, feet—and their mutually dependent relationship are well known in pediatrics and physical therapy. Their foundation is self-touch, which begins in babyhood and is one of the requirements for healthy functioning.

In connection with this, the development of a preferred sidedness (laterality) has long been of interest to developmental psychologists. All complex coordinated movement is based on this principle, and we point this out to the child in the simplest possible way by referring to the hands. Their touching is the paradigm for a back-and-forth subject-object relationship. The child will name other matching twosomes found as part of the human whole: two eyes, two ears, two feet etc. Every paired organ and its functioning carries meaning for the human consciousness and its relationship to the world.

During the lecture cycle given in Torquay Rudolf Steiner suggested an important addition to this concept that goes beyond organic structures and their organization. Now you continue, call a second child forward and say: *When you two walk, you can meet each other and can also touch. You are a twosome.*

Thus the formation of a pair is described as a social and not solely an organic process. This constitutes the transition to the free creation of pairs, where we mentally unite two items into one unit and call them a pair, a two. This process can be viewed as an "absterben" because two stones or two chairs lack the natural intimate relatedness of two hands, feet, or eyes. Our thinking is able to recognize as "two" even items that are connected only by our mental concept of them as belonging together.

The transition to the threesome Steiner carries out as a mere addition: "Somebody else can join the two. With the hands, this cannot be the case. In this way, one can transition to the three for the child." and he draws:

If we want to introduce the three through a structure as well, we could use a family or flower forms that contain the three. But as an organizing principle the three does not have a corollary in human physiology.

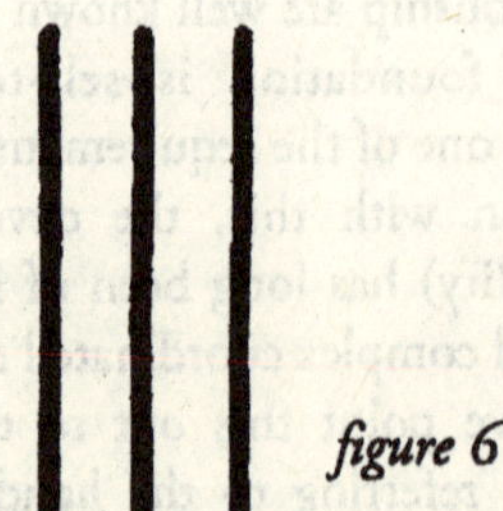

figure 6

Regarding the foursome, Steiner points to an animal: "*You have seen the neighbor's dog; does he walk on just two feet (like* the *child)?* Then the child will come to know in the four strokes (figure 7) the neighbor's dog resting on four legs, and thus it will build up the number out of real life."

For the fivesome we again refer to the hand: *This is a hand. At the end it is divided, and you are all able to count the five fingers, I'm sure, we will use a hand as a symbol for this fivesome.* We show a hand with four fingers close together and the thumb at an angle to form the Roman Numeral for five (figure 8).

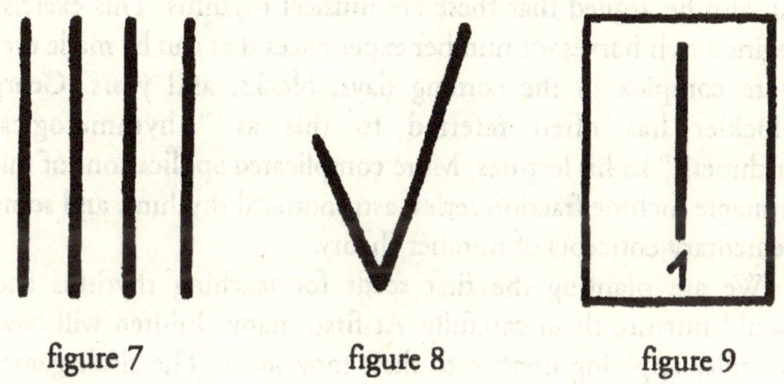

figure 7 figure 8 figure 9

We have now introduced the first numbers as one-ness, twosome, threesome, etc. and have drawn their symbols. The fact that the four is usually written as IV (five-minus-one) should not concern us—it has been and continues to be written like that, as well as the other way.

How much of this introduction actually happens during the first math lesson depends on the flow of the lesson. Even though we recommend a rapid pace such as the one used by Steiner, there has to be time to "digest" the material and we are, after all, limited to 30 minutes for this part of the lesson.

The children can now copy the numbers from one to five into their main lesson books. There should be sufficient space left beneath each Roman Numeral for the Arabic equivalent (figure 9).

Once the numbers have been written into the books, we can begin to address another aspect of numbers: their configuration in time. We could say for example: *Just now you saw the two in your two hands. Now you can listen while I show you the two in another way.* We begin to clap rhythmically ("∪" = short, unstressed, and "—" = long, stressed): ∪ —, ∪ —, ∪ — . . . with great care and attention. Then the children clap also. We show the three ∪ ∪ —, ∪ ∪ —, ∪ ∪ — . . . , and the children also clap that rhythm. We experience the numbers 2 and 3 in this clapping, although it can also be argued that these are musical rhythms. This exercise begins a rich harvest of number experiences that can be made ever more complex in the coming days, blocks, and years. Georg Glöckler has often referred to this as "Rhythmological Arithmetic" in his lectures. More complicated applications of this principle include fraction series, astronomical rhythms, and some elementary concepts of number theory.

We are planting the first seeds for teaching rhythms and should nurture them carefully. At first, many children will have difficulty applying rhythm to their movement. The circle games where music and rhyme support the rhythm are a preparation for this, but the "pure" rhythms will have to be specifically taught in the math lessons. They carry a musical element into math as they penetrate music mathematically.

During this first math lesson we only touch briefly on numbers as rhythms, since we will do more of it every day, and enter one more number area the children are sure to be somewhat familiar with: counting. If we ask: "Who can already count to 20?" many children will raise their hands—but this doesn't mean they can actually do it. But since we know the children, we can let a few capable children count aloud. It is important to end correctly at 20 and not let the child run on. Seemingly small details of form like this can be especially helpful in math, where there is a tendency toward too much activity. For instance, it would be inviting disorder to simply let the children count as far as they can and we would easily lose the rest of the lesson to chaos—unless we then contradict ourselves and tell a child to stop before he/she has finished counting "as far as I can."

Since we have let some of the stronger children count aloud, we can also let some of the weaker ones do so. It is not unusual for children to skip or displace numbers when counting, unless counting was practiced in kindergarten or at home. We should not point out or correct mistakes yet, but it is important to take note if they occur below number 6 or 7. This kind of error could be an early warning sign of a math disability; it will be covered in another chapter.

Counting aloud together concludes this part of the lesson, and the weaker children will be carried by the group activity.

We end the main lesson with a fairy tale that brings the children back "into themselves." Math blocks call forth lots of activity with inner and outer movement, so it is particularly true for the math block that the fairy tale can reestablish balance through its quiet inward mood. "Brother and Sister" is one good example of such a tale.

Overview

If we assume a time limit of 110 minutes for the main lesson, we can establish the following lesson plan, beginning at eight o'clock:

8:00 – 8:10	greeting, morning verse, shortened rhythmic part
8:10 – 8:20	conversation about number work
8:20 – 8:50	the concepts of oneness, twosome, etc. and the first (Roman) numerals
8:50 – 9:00	writing in main lesson books
9:00 – 9:05	optional small break
9:05 – 9:25	numbers as rhythmic configurations in time; counting singly and together
9:25 – 9:45	fairy tale
9:45 – 9:50	snacktime in the classroom, followed by recess outside

The Second Math Lesson

Beginning with the second day, the rhythmic part can resume a normal time of 20 to 30 minutes, though most of this will be dedicated to working with numbers. The crucial experience of numbers, as well as basic math concepts, rests on an inner certainty of our senses of movement and balance. Therefore we try to combine numbers with various kinds of movement, we almost "dance" the numbers, always keeping in mind the two poles of activity: physically moving the numbers and inwardly becoming aware of the movement. The first pole builds and exercises the physical body, trains the sense of balance, and stimulates one's own sense of movement. The other pole is connected to our imagination and the inner activity that takes place there. In our rhythmic work with numbers we have to be ever mindful of both poles. Generally the lesson begins with physical, will-related activities such as stomping, clapping, hopping, speaking, etc. These also develop proper body orientation and large muscle dexterity.

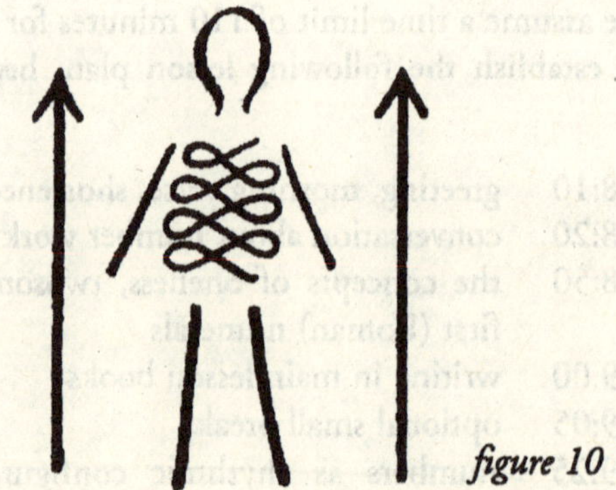

figure 10

We then transition to the more imagination-related activities by using smaller and less obvious movements (e.g., using fingers instead of feet, using either language or movement but not both at once, skipping parts of movements, letting groups listen and speak in turn, varying between group and single activities, and, finally letting the body come to complete quiet). This transition from the will pole to the imagination pole should happen during each lesson, as it is characteristic for the child's overall development. The connecting element is the rhythm. The following is a description of the physiological transition from willing through feeling to thinking.

While developing, the child moves from physical-motor learning to imaginative learning to conceptual learning. All our lessons therefore—with different emphasis as the children get older—"breathe" between the will pole and the imagination pole.

At the end of the rhythmic exercises we invariably make sure to establish a quiet and focused ending mood. One colleague uses this moment to draw a geometric form, for instance a circle or an ellipse, and lets the class correct the form with the utmost concentration until it is perfect. This mood of quiet readiness is necessary for a successful learning phase of the lesson.

We now begin the new learning phase by drawing yesterday's numbers one after the other on the blackboard and asking the children what they mean. Then we ask specific children to draw the signs for the numbers they have already learned, perhaps only into the air so that we can quickly see the result. If we did not cover all the numbers up to five, we continue as described above.

If we have covered all the numbers up to five on the first day, we then introduce the Arabic numbers by stating that grownups usually write numbers differently from the way we learned them yesterday. We also say that this old way is sometimes still used today and that we should therefore also be able to recognize it. We then carefully draw the first Arabic number on the blackboard and let the children draw it into the air. A few children may then draw it on the board and finally everyone writes it into the main lesson book. The numbers 2 and 3 require extra care as they have pointed tips that are not easily drawn. We write the Arabic numbers beneath the Roman Numerals already in the book.

Simply introducing the numbers is not sufficient; they have to be practiced just like the letters in order to acquire motoric certainty. This should be done right away in school but could also be homework: *Write on the next pages the numbers 1 to 5 until you can write them very nicely. Tomorrow you may show me your most beautiful numbers.*

This is not generally very difficult since the form drawing and writing blocks have already practiced this skill. The teacher should carefully consider ahead of time how to write the numbers fluidly and attractively, since this lesson will instill lifelong habits in the children.

Once the numbers have been written into the main lesson books, we can turn to "number guessing" games. We challenge the children to use their various senses in determining numbers. A few examples for the lower grades follow; they should be supplemented and varied according to one's own imagination:

Sense of Hearing: Sounding sticks or other items are hit and the number of hits has to be counted. Or: Several tones are produced, some of them different from others. How many different tones were produced?

Sense of Touch: One child stands in front of the class and is touched with a pencil on the back, the head, or the knees. Or: The child turns away and several fingers are held together; how many? Or the children count stones with their feet while blindfolded.

Sense of Touch and Warmth: A child is blindfolded, and a small group of children walks around the child and shakes his/her hand at every turn. How many children are in the circle?

Sense of Taste and Smell: A child is blindfolded and is offered several samples of different-smelling things, such as cheese, bread, and lemons. How many were bread and how many were lemons?

And how many different kinds of smells were there (3 - lemons, bread and cheese)?

Sense of Vision: A child is shown a number of fingers for a short time only and has to guess how many. Or: How many different colors did I just show you?

We can approach these games with lots of imagination. Their main purpose is to help keep in mind the specific soul orientation of the senses for each child. Also, the children's own sense of movement is stimulated, and it is the one responsible for the formation of number concepts. This playful approach avoids the inflexible connection between a number and a sense impression that results when sticks of a specific color and length are used for each number. The true foundation for the number concept is an inner experience of movement; all fixed ties to outer sense impressions are superfluous and foreign. While it may be true that such ties make it easier to teach and learn numbers, we can disregard these arguments if we value an inner activity and an encounter with the nature of numbers for the child.

After the number guessing game we add just a few number exercises since our time for these during the rhythmic portion of the lesson is limited. We are careful to observe the breathing rhythm for activitivating and calming the children's bodies. A fairy tale concludes the lesson.

The Structure of the First Block

The structure of the second math lesson can serve as a model for all other regular math lessons. At first we introduced and practiced the Roman Numerals up to V according to the method described above. It should be obvious that we are not teaching the first five numbers, which any healthy first grader has already mastered. The learning content is the analytical introduction of the numbers (from the whole to the parts) and the introduction of written symbols for them.

I recommend a rapid introduction of the Arabic numbers. Neither the reciting of numbers nor their writing down on paper is a mathematical activity. The math curriculum has to include both these conventional elements because they are required for communicating, but they should not take up more room than is their due. Therefore, we should not waste time on slowly introducing the written numbers.

The second reason I like to introduce numbers quickly and without pictures (unlike the consonants) is that their pictureless nature reaches toward the musical and rhythmical realms. In anthroposophical terms, we say that numbers are characteristically inspirative and not imaginative. We honor this by practicing numbers rhythmically and musically. In the end, the root of our ability to grasp amounts of spatially arranged items is a movement process.

Counting Beyond 5

figure 11

figure12

Having introduced Roman and Arabic numbers up to five, we now turn to the remaining numbers up to 10. This should generally be accomplished during the first week. For the Roman Numerals we add the second hand and cross it over the first hand to form the 10 (figure 11)

When introducing the Arabic numbers we encounter the problem of place value when adding the second number. We can explain this as follows: *If you have counted as far as you can on your fingers, the way people used to do in olden times, then you imagine a bundle or a sack around the things you have already counted: 10.* (figure 12)

The 0 is the sign for the sack. Two sacks are then 20, etc. If there are more items than 10, they are left over, i.e. 11 or 12 or 13. We actually only write the sign for the sack if there is nothing left over to be counted. (figure 13)

figure12

In this way we gradually begin to write the numbers past 10. The first number counts how often we have counted to 10. The second number counts the amounts of things left over. Later we manage the transition of counting past 100 and 1000 in a similar fashion.

THE MATH OPERATIONS
The Four Processes

The learning goal for the first math blocks is the introduction and practice of the math operations. The process of reaching this goal demands careful attention. If we want to apply Steiner's indications for how soul qualities are reflected in the four operations—addition, subtraction, multiplication, and division—and how they relate to the four temperaments, it is helpful to understand their structure and specific interrelatedness. Accordingly, a few basic explanations appear below as background for the teacher.

The Structure of the Operations

When we add two numbers together, i.e., 7 + 5, 3 + 4, 2 + 3, the two addends differ in their function. The first number is enlarged by the second one. The first addend represents the status quo, the stock we have to work with, while the second addend represents a change in the status quo. We can easily see the difference in this simple example: Let's assume somebody has $1 and receives $1,000,000 as opposed to somebody who has $1,000,000 and is given $1. We notice the difference between the two processes through a change in heart rate alone! Adding 1,000,000 to 1 is obviously not identical to adding 1 to 1,000,000. The symbol for "equals" (=) does not refer to identical processes but to identical end results. As long as we have the operation in front of us, we can clearly see the difference in the role of the addends. This difference can be generalized by using the terms "active," "passive," and "result." The first addend is the given, the number to be enlarged. It is passive. The second addend actively enlarges the first number. Through the operation we find the result. If *p* stands for passive, *a* for active and *r* for result, the following formula symbolizes this process:

$$p + a = r$$

Of these three numbers, two are usually given. Aside from the addition, two other inverse operations ("reversals") are therefore possible: If p and r are given, a can be determined in this manner:

$$p + ? = r \quad \text{or} \quad r \mid p = a?$$

We use the | sign to differentiate this reversal, this finding the difference, from regular subtraction. Questions that clarify this process could include the following:

– The numbers r and p are given. How big is the difference between them?

– p is given. How much is lacking to make up r?

– We had r and are now left with p. How much did we lose?

If, contrary to the above, r and a are given, then p can be determined. This is regular subtraction:

$$? + a = r \quad \text{or} \quad r - a = p?$$

Questions leading into this process could include:

– From r we take away a. How much is left?

– To which number do we have to add a in order to have r?

Obviously there are varied ways these questions could be asked. The point to remember is that the children's thinking processes vary along with the questions. Which questioning process to choose and when is discussed further below. For now we can summarize:

<u>active reversal</u>	<u>operation</u>	<u>passive reversal</u>
	Addition	
Subtraction	$p + a$	Differentiation
$r - a = p$		$r \mid p = a$

We explain subtraction and differentiation as separate processes in this context because in plain addition, taught the usual way, the sum is the same irrespective of the order of the addends (rule of exchange or commutative rule). In complex math this is generally as false as it is in real life (as in the example of $1 versus $1,000,000). The order of steps and events plays a crucial role there.

From the process of addition two steps take us to multiplication:
– 1st step: There are sums with more than two addends

$$r = a + b + c + d + \ldots$$

– 2nd step: Among the sums with several addends are specifically those with identical multiple addends

$$r = p + p + \ldots. + p$$

In this instance we count the addends, determine their number *a* and view *r* as *p* multiplied *a* times:

$$r = a \cdot p \quad \text{or} \quad a \cdot p = r$$

We have created the ***product*** ***r*** out of the ***factors*** ***a*** and ***p***. The difference between *a* and *p* becomes clear when we use specific examples for *p* (and thereby *r* also):

$$12 \text{ feet} = 3 \text{ feet} + 3 \text{ feet} + 3 \text{ feet} + 3 \text{ feet}$$

$$12 \text{ feet} = 4 \cdot 3 \text{ feet}$$

The number 4 counts the amount of identical addends. It is a pure number, as opposed to *r* and *p*, which have units associated with them. Again the equal sign (=) refers to the end results, not to identical processes (where 4 · 3 feet would be identical to 3 · 4 feet), since both result in 12 feet. If we imagine these combinations in board feet, however, the resulting buildings would look quite different!

In the multiplication formula $a \cdot p = r$ the active multiplying factor is *a*, the passive manipulated factor is *p*; *a* is the ***multiplier***, *p* the ***multiplicand***.

Just as was the case with addition, two reversals can be formed out of the multiplication process. The initial factors can be *a* and *r* or *p* and *r* (besides the standard *a* and *p*). If the result *r* and the multiplicand *p* are given, we look for the active multiplier that tells us how many times *p* is *r*. This becomes clear if we imagine two lengths of wood and are finding out how often the shorter one fits into the longer piece. We are measuring the longer piece with the shorter one, and the answer we get expresses the relation between the two. (We are only dealing with whole factors here.) The operation that determines *a* when *r* and *p* are given we label *measuring* or *finding the ratio.* When using unit measurements, the unitless number is the factor.

If the result *r* and the multiplier *a* are given, we are dealing with the standard division process: The whole is divided into identical parts and the size of the parts needs to be determined. Using unit measurements we divide the total size *r* by the pure number *a* and determine *p*, whose unit is identical to *r*.

When measuring or finding the ratio, we write:

$$? \cdot p = r \quad \text{or} \quad r : p = ?$$

The questions leading into this process could look like these:

– What is the ratio between *r* and *p* ?

– Given are the total *r* and one part *p*. How often is *p* contained in *r* ?

– Given is *p*. But the total is supposed to be *r*. How often do we have to use *p* in order to make up *r* ?

For the division process we write:

$$a \cdot ? = r \quad \text{or} \quad \frac{r}{a} = p ?$$

The questions we ask the children could be similar to these:

– *r* is divided into *a* equal parts. How big is one part?

– Which number p, when multiplied with a, results in the total r?

Again, the questions can be posed in various ways to stimulate different thinking processes in the children. The diagram below summarizes the above information:

active reversal	operation	passive reversal
	Addition $p + a$	
Subtraction $r - a = p$		Differentiation $r \mid p = a$
	1st tier of development	
	Multiplication $a \cdot p = r$	
Division $\frac{r}{a} = p$		Finding the ratio $r : p = a$

Again, we define division and finding the ratio separately because standard math teaching does not always differentiate between multiplicand and multiplier. In higher mathematics these processes, just like subtraction and differentiation, differ significantly. We therefore identify these process reversals at this early stage as separate operations.

Beyond multiplication we proceed in 2 more steps to yet another form of calculation, finding the powers.

1st step: We examine multiplication processes containing several multipliers:

$$r = a \cdot b \cdot c \ldots$$

2nd step: Among these there are specific cases where all the multipliers are identical:

$$r = \underbrace{p \cdot p \cdot \ldots \cdot p}_{a}$$

Now we count the factors and thus determine their amount *a*. *r* is then the *a-th* power of *p*. We write:

$$r = p^a \cdot p$$

The number that is "potentized," *p*, is the ***base number; a***, the potentizing number, is the ***exponent***.

The first thing one notices about finding the power is that the base and the exponent can no longer be interchanged at will, as the following example shows:

$$3^2 = 3 \cdot 3 = 9 \quad \text{but} \quad 2^3 = 2 \cdot 2 \cdot 2 = 8$$

As a result reversing the process does not work the same way either, and we determine the reversals by finding the third number when two of them are given, i.e. *r* and *a* are given; what is *p* ? Or *r* and *p* are given; what is *a* ?

If *r* and *p* are given, we are looking for the exponent *a* which potentizes *p* and results in *r* :

$$p^? = r$$

This operation, which asks for the exponent, is called ***logarithm finding*** and is written this way:

$${}_p\log r = a$$

This is read like this: logarithm of *r* to the base *p* .

The other reversal, the active one, is finding the root. Here we ask for *p* which, when potentized with *a*, equals *r*

$$?^a = r$$

Solving the equation for *p* we write:

$$\sqrt[a]{r} = p$$

and read: the *a-th* root of *r*.

The introductory questions for these reversed processes of potentizing follow:

For logarithms:

- What is the logarithm of r to the base p ?
- Given are the whole r and the base number p. How many factors p result in r ?
- p is given. Form r as a power of p. How often do we have to use p as a factor?

For finding the root:

- The result r is to be divided into a product of a equal factors. How big does the single factor p have to be ?
- What size p, when potentized by a, results in the total r?

These questions could be constructed in other ways.

The diagram on the next page summarizes the nine operations we have described:

active reversal	operation	passive reversal
	Addition	
	$p + a$	
Subtraction		Differentiation
$r - a = p$		$r \mid p = a$
	1st tier of development	
	Multiplication	
	$a \cdot p = r$	
Division		Finding the ratio
$\frac{r}{a} = p$		$r : p = a$
	2nd tier of development	
	Potentizing	
	$p^a = r$	
Finding the root		Finding the logarithm
$\sqrt[a]{r} = p$		$_p\log r = a$

This concludes the explanation of the elementary operations and their interconnections. One could ask if this diagram could not be expanded to include yet higher processes, and this is possible in theory although more and more algebraic rules are lost along the way. We saw the beginning of this where the commutative rule no longer applies to potentizing. Unless new applications demand this type of analysis, it will remain unused (although modern math and physics do deal with non-commutative and non-associative structures).

Having created this expansion into nine operations, we can then reduce them again:

1. Since the commutative rule applies only to addition and multiplication, we can identify subtraction and differentiation as well as division and ratio finding in the manner described above.

2. By introducing negative numbers, we can formally replace subtraction with addition of negative numbers, like this:

$$a - b \quad \text{becomes} \quad a + (-b)$$

3. Similarly, by introducing fractions we can replace division with multiplying by the inverse fraction:

$$a : b = a \cdot {}^{1}/_{b}$$

4. Exponents that are fractions show that finding the root can be traced back to finding the power:

$$\sqrt[a]{r} = p$$

We now show the two-step reduction process from 9 operations to 7 and then to 4:

Original operation	1st reduction	2nd reduction
Addition	Addition	Addition
Differentiation	———	———
Subtraction	Subtraction	———
Multiplication	Multiplication	Multiplication
Finding the ratio	———	———
Division	Division	———
Potentizing	Potentizing	Potentizing
Logarithm	Logarithm	Logarithm
Finding the root	Finding the root	———

After this excursion into the field of mathematics we now turn again to the introductory math lessons in the first grade and to their content, the four basic operations. In a further step we then show their place in the overall operations blueprint.

Introducing the First Operation in Grade 1

We introduced the numbers by going from the whole to the parts and continue this analytical process in teaching the operations. We examine one whole (unit) and then grasp its component structure. For instance, in the learning part of one of the first days of the math block, we can recall the five by saying and showing: "Look, this is a hand. Notice how the five fingers grow: they form a four and a one. Together they are five fingers, but divided they are four and one. Taken together again they are five."

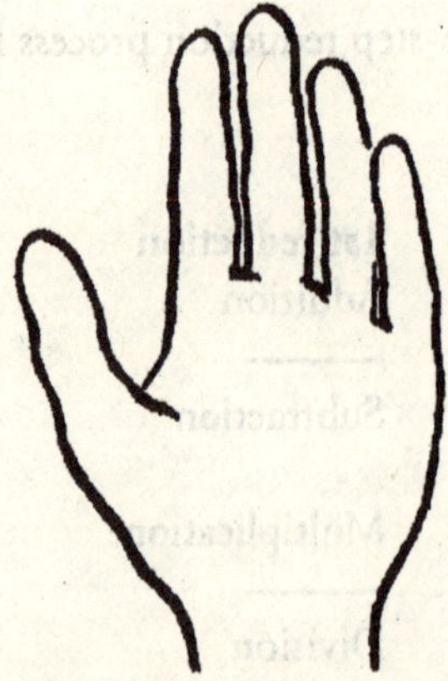

figure 14

We move our fingers accordingly while we speak. Then we spread the fingers and show what else the five can consist of, i.e. 1 and 2 and 2; together 1 and 2 and 2 form five again.

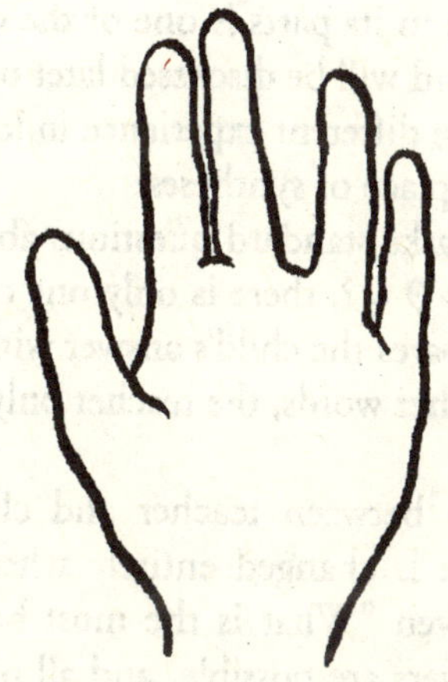

figure 15

Then we ask the children to show different fives themselves. In this way we introduce the first math operation as an additive structuring, as an additive analysis of a number. We can recombine the parts (synthesis) and form the original number again. This structuring (analyzing) and recombining (synthesizing) we can apply to various numbers.

To write down this process we simply place a number onto the center of the page and write the various possible combinations beneath it:

7
1 5 1
3 4
2 3 2
1 2 1 2 1
6 1

Going from a whole to its parts is one of the crucial processes of Waldorf pedagogy and will be discussed later on. At this point we want to highlight the different experience in learning math when analyses are used in place of syntheses.

When a teacher asks standard questions about addition, such as $7 + 3 = ?$ or $2 + 9 = ?$, there is only one correct answer. The teacher simply compares the child's answer with the solution s/he already knows. In other words, the teacher only checks for "right" or "wrong."

The relationship between teacher and class as well as the working atmosphere is changed entirely when the teacher asks "What is 16?" or even "What is the most beautiful 16?" How many different answers are possible, and all of them are correct! Here are a few samples:

16
8 8
4 4 4 4
3 4 2 4 3
1 5 1
1 2 4
1 2 3 4 3 2 1

The teacher has to listen in an entirely different way to the children's answers—and double check all answers mentally! If the given number is not too small, the teacher will be busily calculating instead of just checking for right or wrong, and feel that each answer is a new challenge.

Consequences of this Teaching Method

Through the application of this method, the child learns something basic: a question can (or even has to) have many possible answers. The child's individual view shapes his/her answer. Those teachers who know their children well can recognize just how much of the child's nature reveals itself in the answers. Often the whole class is amazed by one child's ingenuity. However, this freedom of selecting one's individual answer is tied to the group's assessment of the answer. We are free in our unique view of solutions, but as soon as we make them public, everyone can judge their usefulness and truth. And in this we find a basic principle for our method: from inside ourselves as well as from our environment, problems present themselves. They almost always require more than one solution, since each new solution we think of creates more intricate layers demanding more solutions.

Let's take the hypothetical case of a House of Representatives (trained in this method) debating the unemployment problem. Instead of espousing the sole truth in the form of the party line, the Representatives would gather the most diverse points of view: young people, seniors, employees, the self-employed, single parents, the handicapped, etc. would all be asked to contribute to the discussion, as well as bankers and automation specialists.

Ready answers to problems prevent us from seeing the true variety of possible solutions and the result is narrow decisions based on insufficient input from others. The decision makers try to elicit this input through public hearings, expert testimony, round table discussions, and so on. But too many of these attempts fail because those involved may never have learned to create diversity in their own thinking. We should also ponder a statement frequently heard in this context: "We can't change the status quo; this is simply the way things are. After all, 2 + 2 = 4, and we can't change that, either." What kind of math instruction are we dealing with when people refer to math as a metaphor for unalterable circumstances?! If everyone had learned as a matter of course that 2 + 2 = 4, but so are 1 + 3 and 1 + 1 + 1 + 1, we would not subconsciously "know" that math represents the unyielding and unchangeable forces in life. Instead, our method of teaching the whole and then its components can initiate experiences of individual freedom and cooperative thinking.

Analysis and Synthesis

The method described above can also be viewed within a larger context. If we look for analysis and synthesis in today's world, we find them in organic growth and technical production processes. A technical item such as a car is produced in separate parts which are later assembled through a series of (synthetic) stages. Organic growth is completely different: from the initial uniform mass of cells more complex structures emerge through a process of inner differentiation of both form and function.

If we try to interchange both processes for clarity's sake, we have to imagine an organism produced as separate organs and later put together, while a car would grow from a blob of fiberglass cells into the familiar combination of tires, motor, spark plugs, etc. This hypothetical reversal emphasizes the differences between the two processes.

One attribute of analytical-organic growth is that each of the parts is related to the whole. Understanding one organ of a certain organism (e.g., a kidney or spleen) is only possible when the whole organism is known. This means we have to develop holistic thinking that can guide us from the whole to the parts. The whole has to inform all knowledge about any part of an organic whole or, as Maturana and Varela put it, an autopoietic system. How much these forms of thinking are needed when dealing with living systems is best illustrated by the current environmental crisis. For the past 150 years, we have applied mechanistic thinking to changing the earth. We have succeeded in treating it like a dead thing.

This crisis should more commonly be viewed as a result of underdeveloped thinking, especially by concerned teachers. We need to go beyond moralizing reminders to treat nature as a living being. Waldorf pedagogy offers concrete methods for developing and nurturing new ways of thinking. (See also Steiner's *The Science of Knowing*, especially the chapters about organic and inorganic nature.).

When an inventor conceives of the idea for a new invention, his thinking about the idea and its possible realization is a process of organic growth. An invention is after all never put together out of parts but is first discovered as a meaningful whole and then the steps toward actually building the item can be taken. Many of the first inventors were holistic thinkers who only secondarily developed an interest in the necessary details their projects required.

These explanations of the two thinking processes are not meant to imply a bias toward either one. Both synthetic and analytical thinking can be appropriate, depending on the situation. However, since synthetic thinking is so prevalent and often destructive in our culture, analytical thinking should at least be given equal weight.

In order to nurture both forms of thinking in our teaching, we have to keep in mind that the child's physical body belongs to the organic realm and that the first conscious learning steps happen when the inner organic differentiation is coming to an end (See Kranich et al., 1992). Through anthroposophical pedagogy we attempt to connect the thinking forms learned in math with the termination of the bodily differentiation processes and to school synthetic thinking as a kind of reflection or mirror image.

The Elementary Operations

After we have introduced addition as a structuring of a given whole and touched on the synthesis of the parts to again form a whole, we practice both operations with many different materials, such as stones, chestnuts, wood chips, etc. But we need to find practical examples for applying the procedures, and short math stories provide situations requiring calculations and containing problems the children can solve.

Having begun with analytical and synthetical addition, we want to transition to the other operations fairly quickly. For the differentiation operation we can use the popular "finger guessing" game already mentioned with the number games: we hold some of the child's fingers together when the child is not looking and ask how many we are holding. This is at first a good exercise to bring consciousness into the fingers. (See Kranich, 1970, in connection with math dysfunction.) Then we pose a second question: *"How many fingers am I not holding?"* The child can find the answer to this the same way s/he came to the first answer, but can also begin with the whole, all 10 fingers, and find the difference between that and the 6 fingers being held—then 4 fingers are not being held.

The actual finding of this difference can be the main topic one day during the third week of the first math block when we tell the story of a child who is sent to the store to buy apples. The mother gives the child 10 quarters. The apples cost four quarters and the child still has six quarters. While running home quickly with the bag of apples in one hand and the coins in the other, the child hears a tinkling sound and stops to count the quarters. There are only two quarters left in the child's hand, and some coins are lying on the sidewalk. How many quarters does the child have to look for on the sidewalk?

If we don't know how many items we are looking for we don't know when to stop looking and could spend all day on the sidewalk. So it is good to know how much we have lost when we look for something. Then we can search much more effectively.

The actual subtraction can be discussed as a 2nd step. If the child has lost four quarters of the six, two remain. The first instance (how many have we lost?) asks for the number *a* that changes, while the whole *r* and the new status quo *p* are given. (2 = 6 - ? or 6 - 2 = ?) The second instance subtracts the loss *a* from the whole r and finds the new situation p (6 - 4 = 2). The first case deals with the difference between two given situations, the second case with the result of a subtraction.

We move on to measuring or finding the ratio, where we also describe a relationship between two given amounts. We prepare for this early on in the rhythmic part of the lesson by rhythmically introducing rows of numbers. For example, by emphasizing the multiples of 3 and gradually letting the numbers in between fade away, we let the row stand alone.

Having prepared this row rhythmically, we can also portray it spatially: we create a "creek" with "stepping stones" so that we can cross the creek with 12 steps. If we use increments of 2, we need six steps, increments of 3 need only four steps, etc. The total number of steps should ideally be divisible by many numbers.

In this task we relate two different numbers of steps to each other, the original number (i.e., 12) of steps and the step increment number (i.e., 2). Then we count the steps. Thus we build up, in a multiplicative structure, the relation 12 : 2 = 6. The numbers on the left are lengths measured by the original step from stone to stone. The number on the right is the (pure) ratio that states the factor of steps to the whole. We determine this factor not by looking at the compared lengths but by concentrating on our activity of stepping.

We follow such exercises with a transition to spatial relations. We put several items on the floor and let the class determine their number by counting. Then we choose an appropriate partial amount and ask how many times this amount is contained within the whole. We are again comparing two similar numbers: amounts of items. The relation is a pure number, not an amount of things. Determining the structure and synthetically combining parts are opposite processes. For instance, if the whole is 12 and the partial amount is 4, the answer to the question "How often is 4 contained in 12?" is: 3 times. Synthetically speaking, we reverse this statement and say: 3 times 4 is 12.

In another paragraph below we will talk about another important task, the restructuring of a number whose multiplicative structure we have determined, so that multiplier and multiplicand appear reversed. For example, having determined the structure $12 = 2 \cdot 6$, the reversal would state $12 = 6 \cdot 2$. In the first grade, these are not explained by the commutative rule, but are taught differently through different thinking processes.

We introduce another form of multiplication by describing the product content, but defining it only through the factors given. "Going from the whole to the parts" therefore does not just refer to giving a result and then analyzing its components, but also to stating a goal and then determining what steps to take to reach it. The question then is: in which number *r* (described by content) is a given number *p* contained *a* times? An example follows in the next chapter. Immediately following this we turn to standard division as the reverse of the above procedure:

$$\frac{r}{a} = p$$

without formally introducing the symbol for "divided by."

Operations and Temperaments

This section assumes a thorough knowledge of the temperaments and their anthroposophical underpinnings as described in *The Foundation of Human Experience* by Rudolf Steiner.

Equally essential is knowledge of the members of the human being, since their varying dominance or weakness create the individual temperament structure. Therefore each statement characterizing a given temperament only applies to an ideal prototype that doesn't exist as such. These typical descriptions are used to increase understanding for individual temperament profiles and to assess dominant qualities accurately. In any normal class we find a few children whose behavior shows an obvious dominant temperament. But most of the children fall somewhere in the middle between the temperaments, especially since the group and the current activity can bring out one temperament above others. Also, there are people with a phlegmatic build, sanguine perception, and choleric thinking, etc.

In describing the operations and their relation to the temperaments we refer primarily to the explanation Rudolf Steiner gave in the 4th lecture of *Discussions with Teachers* which is reproduced in its entirety in Appendix 2. Each temperament appears twice, once in a dominant and once in a supporting role. The four temperaments are arranged in a pattern that pairs each with its opposite:

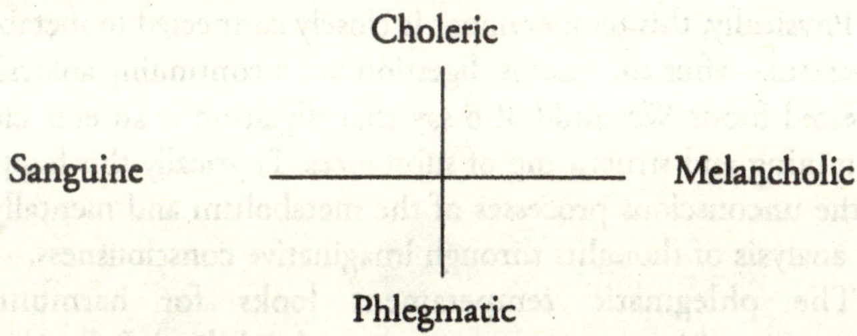

The relationship between a temperament and its opposite is a recurring theme in the chapters below.

Math for the Phlegmatic Temperament

The main tasks we present to phlegmatics include grasping the whole, determining the amount of equal items combined within it, and additive structuring of these items. The drawing symbolizing this process is on the next page.

This surrounding of items forming a whole and then analyzing them are, on different levels, the typical gestures of the phlegmatic.

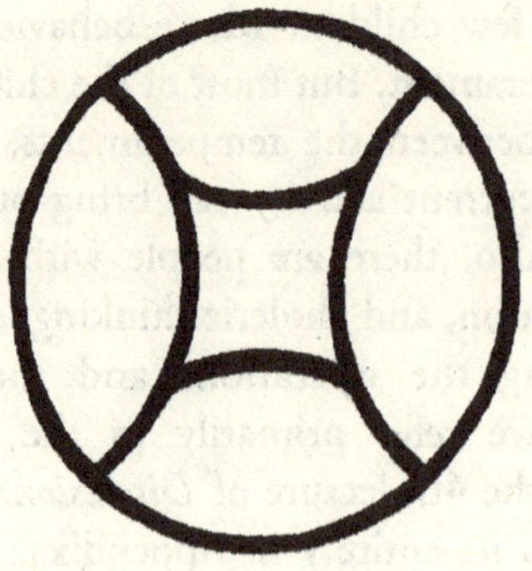

figure 16

Physically, this temperament is closely connected to metabolic processes—after all, what is digestion but a continuing analysis of ingested food? We could also say that digestion is an ever closer examining and structuring of substances. Physically this happens in the unconscious processes of the metabolism and mentally in the analysis of thoughts through imaginative consciousness.

The phlegmatic temperament looks for harmonious interaction with others on an emotional (soul) level. Belonging to a group or being cast out of it is crucial. Responsible application of this principle can contribute positively to group dynamics, since inner organization and a harmonious balance of power call forth phlegmatic tendencies in a group.

Synthetically recombining the parts found through analysis demands a more conscious effort directed at the outside world. Here choleric nuances of the soul appear. In teaching, we therefore ask a child with phlegmatic tendencies to analyze and turn to a child of the opposite temperament to carry out the synthesis back to the whole.

Math for the Melancholic Temperament

The melancholic's task is to find the difference when the whole and the remainder are given. This activity mirrors his emotional (soul) experience of him/herself in relation to the world, as the melancholic temperament tends to perceive the difference between itself and the world. It is especially conscious of its own shortcomings compared to a high ideal. Noticing other people's abilities creates both this high ideal and the painful feeling of one's own inability. Naturally, everyone experiences this difference once in a while, but the melancholic tinge shows in the reaction to this experience of the difference between a high ideal and one's own self assessment. This reaction should not be mistaken for a depressive mood. The inwardly very active melancholic is frequently motivated by this experience to try harder and develop his/her skills further.

When a child with melancholic soul qualities has completed the process of finding the difference between whole and remainder, we let a sanguinely oriented child solve the same problem as an active subtraction. Where the melancholic calculated $r \mid p = a$, the sanguine executes the opposite movement in the subtraction: $r - a = p$.

Math for the Sanguine Temperament

The breathing rhythmical element is important in tasks for the sanguine temperament. Among the operations, finding the ratio with its multiplicative structure seems best. The sanguine lives strongly in the relationships to his/her surroundings and to the activities that can be developed therein. What is interesting are not the objects themselves, but the possibilities for action they present.

We pointed out in preceding sections how in calculating with unit measurements, the ratio is found as a pure number, not a unit measurement. Thus two lengths can have the same ratio to each other as two widths, for instance. This detachment from the physical is related to the sanguine experience. The lightness and flexibility characteristic of the soul gesture of the sanguine are the result of the ability to detach from the physical. Where this is not successful, sadness descends like a heavy cloud in front of the usually happy mood and the swing Goethe described as "gloriously happy—grievously sad" results.

Once again, the opposite temperament is called on to perform the reversal of the operation. The melancholic is asked to restructure by interchanging the multiplier and the multiplicand. Where the sanguine was given r items as a whole, told that p part of the items was separate and then asked to find multiplier a, the melancholic is told that a part the size of a is separate and is asked to find p (which is now the multiplier).

This restructuring process is formally absolutely clear since the commutative rule applies. When dealing with items, however, the qualitative difference between the respective multiplier and multiplicand is immediately apparent.

It seems questionable to use geometrically structured patterns as illustrations since the above mentioned difference between multiplier and multiplicand, for instance, could easily be overlooked. What is spatially clear is not necessarily truly understood.

The child has accomplished much when it is able to rearrange a previously ordered whole. In actual applications—as already stated—the factors are not generally interchangeable. This restructuring then requires a special inner activity and mobility, which is both especially easy and necessary for the melancholic due to his tendency to cling to previously established thought patterns.

There is an exercise in form drawing that shows what is demanded of the melancholic child: the form on the left is drawn by the teacher. Then a child with melancholic qualities is asked to draw the same form but to color only where the teacher did not and vice versa. The child is once again required to change the status quo through inner activity, in this case by forming the negative of the given picture.

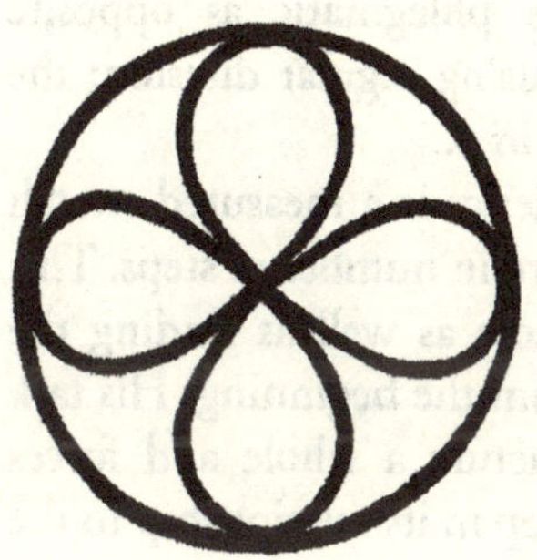

figure 17

Math for the Choleric Temperament

In order to understand Rudolf Steiner's remarks about math for the choleric child, it is helpful to remind oneself of the characteristic attributes of this temperament. Positively, it expresses itself in initiative and creative force, founded on certain self-confidence and trust in one's own abilities. However, this certainty and trust can overestimate what is realistically possible. One example of this is the character of Bottom in Shakespeare's *Midsummer Night's Dream.* When the roles for the play are handed out, he thinks he would be the best player in every role and would like to portray them all at the same time, if he could. He is convinced that he is the very best actor. Such behavior can certainly be found outside the theater as well.

In planning math for this temperament, it must be emphasized that the choleric is conscious of the entirety of a situation. The whole and its contents are understood, but the multitude of functions within and their interplay is not yet clear. In math we utilize this by describing a product *r* by content and giving the factors *p* and *a*. In arithmetic, we ask: "In what number *r* is *p* contained *a* times?"

When the solution is found, the phlegmatic as opposite temperament reverses the process by using regular division: the number *r*, divided into *a* parts, results in *p*.

Another exercise especially for cholerics is a measured stretch of ground that has to be walked in a certain number of steps. This requires correct assessment of the whole as well as finding the exact measure for the very first step from the beginning. His task addresses the choleric's ability to structure a whole and forces him/her to view consciously the first step in its relationship to the whole.

Conclusions

Connecting soul tendencies with math operations trains the children's flexibility in restructuring number relations as well as their attention for one another and specifically their temperament opposites. The teacher develops his/her own inner flexibility to a high degree—a difficult undertaking, although it is easier than some teachers thought before they tried it in their work with children. The greatest benefit of this work is the fact that the teacher gains an appreciation of each operation in a context of colorful emotion, and the children learn this as well.

This emotional context enables the children to decide quickly which is the appropriate operation in any given situation. Insecurities in this area often appear later if the characteristic differences between the operations have not been fully experienced. A calculator suggests exactly the kind of sameness we do not want to impress upon the children: a push of the button results in any one of the operations. We therefore have to train the children's ability to perceive the inner character of the operations independently.

There seems to be no hard and fast rule about when to use which operation, other than in skillbuilding exercises. The choice must therefore happen intuitively, the way we connect a concept with an experience. This is possible when the operations have been experienced as differentiated from one another and the ability to analyze a problem clearly has been developed.

Before one can logically structure an operation, one has to have experienced that which is to be structured. What type of experience should it be ? This has been a question for knowledge theorists and developmental psychologists. We try to answer it with the method already described: the experiential foundation for math concepts is the inner experience of movement.

The math operations point in different ways to the movement gestures with which we structure the numbers we experience as inner movement. These movement gestures are related to our body experiences. When finding a ratio we inwardly grasp our rhythmic processes, when additively structuring we sense the relatively independent organs, when finding a difference we experience the lower human being (metabolic/limb system) staying back in relation to the upper (nerve/sense system), and when creating a multiplicatively structured whole we penetrate with our will the whole body as a movement organism.

Overview

Adding

$p + a = r$

Phlegmatic: Additive analytical structuring of a number. What is r? or how can you divide up r? $r = a + b + c + \ldots$ (Choleric: Active synthetic addition: $a + b + c + \ldots = r$)

Finding the difference:

$r \mid p = a$

Melancholic: Given are the whole and the rest: there were r, now only p are left. What was lost? or what do we have to take away in order to be left with p?

Subtracting:

$r - a = p$

(Sanguine: Active subtracting. If I subtract a from r, p is left: $r - a = p$)

Multiplication

$a \cdot p = r$

Choleric: Determining a number out of its multiplicative structure: in which number is p contained a times? $? \, r = a \cdot p$

Finding the ratio

$r : p = a$

Sanguine: Given is the whole r and part p. We are looking for the muliplier a: You have r. How often does it contain the part p? (Melancholic: And how is it if the part is the size of a? Restructuring as in forming a negative.)

Division

$\frac{r}{a} = p$

(Phlegmatic: Active dividing. If I divide r into parts, I am left with parts the size of p: $r/a = p$)

Finding the power

$p^a = r$

Logarithm

${}_p\log r = a$

Finding the root

$\sqrt[a]{r} = p$

A Math Story with Something for Each Temperament

By telling little stories we can introduce the children to the skills to be learned, although we cannot invent a new story for each task. Instead, we simply vary the situation described by asking questions such as: "*And how would it be if. . . ?*" Then we give different numbers for a similar situation. It is best to avoid asking the same questions for a given task over and over again, or to memorize little verses. If the tasks have been thoroughly learned, they can be practiced even if jumbled. This requires a high degree of flexibility on the teacher's part, and the children are then challenged to both determine the correct numbers for the situation and, most importantly, to determine the correct operation. An example of such a story follows:

There was a farm family who lived in the mountains. They did not have an easy life and all family members had to work as hard as they could. Even the children, of which there were three and later more, had to help out as soon as they were able. The father took care of the cows, milked them morning and night, helped the mother make cheese, and repaired the barn and house, which was often necessary in the spring after the snow melted. The mother did the housework, planted a big vegetable garden, made cheese from the cow's milk, and did many other things. The grandfather took care of the goats and sheep, the grandmother of the chickens, and the children helped everyone: they looked for the eggs the chickens always hid outside instead of in the nest in the coop, they picked berries, and they carried firewood for the house and the dairy. When it was haying time, the whole family went up to the pastures where the father and grandfather had mowed the hay and raked or turned the fresh hay so that it would dry quickly. The quicker the sun dried the hay, the better it smelled like sun and flowers, and the cows and goats and sheep would eat it in their pens in the winter when the snow was very high outside.

In this way or somewhat like this, we can give the children glimpses into various situations of life and work. Then we continue:

In the valley below the farm there was a village, where the church was, and the baker and several craftsmen lived. Some farmers also lived in the village, but most of the farmers lived in the mountains around the village, just like this family did. It was an hour's walk to go down to the valley, and the father went once a week to sell their cheese to a store. He also bought things they could not make themselves, such as tools and nails, needles and pots, salt (rock salt for the goats, too) and most importantly, bread and flour, since wheat did not grow very well at all where they lived.

The schoolhouse was also in the village. William, the oldest boy had just turned 7 and was going to the school for the first time. His sister Rebecca was almost 5, and Martin, the youngest, was 2. Now that William was in school, he could do something very useful for his family.

You see, his father did not always go into the village on the same day, and the baker was also a farmer and only baked bread twice a week. If the father went down on a non baking day, the family did not eat bread for a week. Sometimes the mother went into the village to buy things that were needed, and usually took William and Rebecca with her. Maybe you are thinking: But that's too far to walk for such little children, going down the mountain for an hour and up again for one and a half hours! But mountain farm children are used to it. Both children carried backpacks. William carried two loaves of bread home in his, and Rebecca carried apples to eat and her doll.

But now that William was in school and walked to the village every day, he could bring home a loaf or whatever else was needed in his school backpack, and this was a big help to the family.

As time passed, all the children started school, and Mary and Sebastian were born. They were still at home at the time that I'm now telling about, and the bigger children, William, Rebecca, and

Martin, had long ago taken over the bread buying and carrying as their job. They each had big backpacks that could hold many things, and they were always full, because the bigger the family got, the more bread they ate, and William, who was now 12, could eat as much as a grown up. On Fridays when they bought bread, they always had to think about the same question: How many loaves does each one carry? Most of the time they bought 7 loaves, one for each day of the week, but sometimes they had some left and only bought 6, or they bought 8. It was obvious that Martin could not carry as much as Rebecca and William, since he was younger, but he did not want to be called a wimp, either. So how do you think they divided up the loaves?

Now we can calculate the possibilities with the class. The amount of loaves and the number of children carrying them can be varied.

This example is chosen in such a way that the unequal loads are fair because of the age difference among the children. This is important, since an example with unequal amounts of treats would result in protests from the class, and rightfully so. Examples that contain sweets or toys are usually aimed at the children's desire for them and should be eliminated. In my experience, they do not elicit lasting attention from the children anyway.

We now turn to the children with sanguine tendencies and continue:

Going to school is very difficult for the mountain children. They experience sun and rain and snow and wind much more intensely than city children. In winter, they can ski down the mountain but have to push back up through the snow in the afternoon. In spring, it is dangerous because of all the water from the snow melt running down every hill and the creeks flooding the path. In order to walk across without getting wet feet, they used to throw stones down to step on, close enough together so that even the younger ones could cross the creek. At one point they needed 12 stones to cross.

We now draw the path, the creek flooding it and the 12 stepping stones on the floor with chalk.

The bigger children didn't need to step on every stone to get across, they could jump over some. How many jumps would it take them if they stepped on every other stone?

The class can now do this with the help of the drawing on the floor. We can then ask about every third stone, etc. Beginning with the 12 as a whole and the size of the step as a part of the whole, we determine the multiplier, the number of steps. We then write the product and its factors in pairs on the blackboard:

the whole
12

step size	**number of steps**
1	12
2	6
3	4
4	3
6	2
12	1

By varying the whole, we multiplicatively analyze the different numbers and begin to learn something about their difference.

To practice multiplication/division, we can continue like this:

When it was almost Easter time, the mother's sister and her son wrote to say they would visit at Easter. The whole family was very happy about this, since they rarely saw other people in their mountains, and since they would be able to do many things with their relatives. Altogether there would be 2 grandparents, 7 family members, and 2 guests, which makes 11 people. They discussed who should sleep where and what they would do with the guests. One thing they all wanted to do was paint eggs, and they also wanted to bake cakes and order special yeast donuts from the baker. And since they had to order these ahead of time, they needed to know how many to order. They wanted 2 donuts for every person, so how many did they order? Also, they wanted to color 4 eggs for each child, and the mother discussed this with the grandmother. How many eggs would the grandmother have to save for painting?

To teach children how to find the difference, we tell this story:

On the Saturday before Easter, Rebecca offered to walk to the village and bring back the donuts they had ordered. The cousin went along, and they had a good time running and jumping down the path. They bought some other things the mother needed and then stopped at the bakery to pick up their order of donuts. They took turns carrying the backpack up the hills, but Rebecca turned out to be stronger than the cousin since she did this every day. When they got home and counted the donuts onto the table, they found only 15 donuts, but they had ordered 22 donuts. "Didn't you tell the baker? asked the mother. "Yes, I did." said Rebecca. "And you two didn't eat any of the donuts, did you?" asked the mother and looked into their eyes. "No, promise we didn't!" said both children, and since they were very honest children, the mother knew they were telling the truth.

They all looked at each other and didn't know what to say. But then the mother looked at the backpack again and noticed that the seam was ripped, and just then one of the children came running and said, "There are donuts all over the grass!" and all the children went to gather up the donuts. How many would they have to find to have all 22 together again?

As with the other stories, we can vary the numbers and the situations and add questions for the opposite temperaments at opportune moments.

Introducing Operation Symbols

The four symbols (+, - , x, :) can be introduced in a pictorial way that leaves some of the process they stand for still visible, as opposed to the pictureless introduction of the numbers themselves. Every teacher has to find an appropriate way to create the kind of joyful atmosphere where children can come to love abstract symbols. For instance, the plus sign can remind us of a child putting together the two numbers: 4 + 5. One colleague used a story of a fox who steals geese to introduce the minus sign (–). You can only see the foxy tail – because he runs away so fast with his stolen goose. The multiplication sign can remind us of the steps the children had to take to cross the creek: 4 x 3 represents 4 steps of 3 stones each. The division symbol can be remembered from the finding of the ratio of steps to stones, when the older children can take fewer and bigger steps in the story of the farm children: : the lower dot is a stone the child jumps over, the higher dot is the jump.

Remembering the activity these symbols represented helps to color them for the soul. Being able to distinguish the processes helps the child know which process to choose when it is not obvious.

MEMORY FORMATION

One of the most important tasks of the first math lessons is the thorough training of memory. The field of psychology has researched a variety of aspects of memory formation which are all important in their own context. Here we have chosen to highlight one aspect Rudolf Steiner developed in a lecture where he pointed to the different forms of memory during different stages of the cultural evolution. In the oldest culture of India a *local memory* was present, and places where important events had taken place were marked with stones or in other ways to remind people of the event when they entered the space. We can observe this connection between place and repetition of activity in small children, where places will call forth the memory of what took place. Be that the home or less familiar surroundings, the child remembers and wants to do it again.

Later the *rhythmic memory* was developed. It is closely related to language. In Middle Eastern cultures to this day learning of sacred texts is based on repeating what a teacher says. Also, we learn verses and songs easiest within a spoken context and frequently can only remember them within that context. Children of preschool age learn many things this way that they remember for life.

Today the *memory of time* is the operational one in our culture. Everything we have learned and can consciously recall we owe to it. It allows us to store facts and processes, and with the concepts we thus gain we can be inwardly active in the conception of new ideas.

This last form of memory is what Rudolf Steiner refers to when he repeatedly stresses the importance of nurturing the children's memory growth in the context of math lessons. In anthroposophical terms, the development of this form of memory is closely related to the freeing of the ether body from the realm of the head around the time of the change of teeth. The structure of the physical organs is almost complete, and a part of the etheric forces is available for the soul to be used in the free formation of ideas and memory.

Jean Piaget described a stage of (inner) concrete operations, which is an expression of these changes taking place when the child is ready to enter school. The children's imaginary space is now qualitatively different, and they can move around in it to gain convictions about the outer world, such as the fact that volume remains constant even when dimensions change. Memory development enables the I to take hold of these forces, and they have to be guided or the child's imagination remains random and associative without connection to the will. Math lessons offer the perfect vehicle for this guidance in the form of times table drills.

Developmentally, the child already has access to the rhythmic memory, while the memory of time or of the head is formed through our lessons. We can therefore introduce the times tables rhythmically but have to engrave it into the head memory through effort. Addition tables (sums between 1+1 and 10+10) also address the memory of time directly.

Introducing Addition Tables

The child learns addition during the first math block according to the method described above. Beginning with the result, the whole is structured additively and then synthetically added back together. When additively structuring, sums of two numbers occupy a special position. For example, learning the number 7, we write on the board and in the children's main lesson books (even before introducing the + sign) the parts of the sum in orderly rows:

	7	
6		1
5		2
4		3
3		4
2		5
1		6

We practice these by rote until the children know them securely. To that end, we cover or erase one column and point to one of the numbers that are left. The children then name the missing addend. Certain children are even able to name two or three numbers that would add up to 7, but in this exercise we are emphasizing the structuring into two parts.

There are two other drills we can use for each single number. If we are practicing "+2", for instance, we let the children separate the numbers in such a way that the second number is 2. In other words, when we say "5," the children will say "3+2." During the course of the first grade, these drills can be shortened so that only the unknown first addend is named, (for example, we point to 5 and the children say "3" and so forth).

In another (synthetic) drill, the task is to add 2 to the number given, for example, when "5" is said, the answer is "7," 5 + 2 = 7. Here as well the drill can be shortened in order to teach the children to calculate quickly.

When introducing the first drill, we can say "We are practicing the 'and-two.' I think of a number. To this number I have already added 2, and you have to tell me which number I was thinking of." Then I say 7 and the children say 5, and so on. For the second drill, I say "Now you have to add 2 to the number I tell you." When I say 4, the children say 6, and so on.

The children can also "pass on" a problem or practice these drills in groups. The essential point is that the children should no longer need to calculate at the end of these drills, or count two numbers more, but that they have mastered simple additions and know them confidently by heart, securely anchored within the memory.

Having learned the addition tables to 10 + 10 by heart, there should be no difficulty in the drills of "complete to 10." The kind of addition that is often taught, such as:

$$7 + 8 = 7 + (3 + 5) = (7 + 3) + 5 = 10 + 5 = 15$$

is an obstacle rather than a help for a smooth calculation flow if the addition tables are known by heart.

Introducing Multiplication Tables

The times tables grow out of rhythmic work with numbers. Right from the start, we begin to differentiate numbers by saying them loudly or quietly and varying the movements we use. This leads to structured rows of numbers where every other (or every third or fourth, etc.) number is emphasized, and the times tables follow. Knowing them well means that the children can not only recite them by heart but that they develop great flexibility in using them in mixed drills as described above. Reciting the tables as a class or individually is never enough by itself. The following exercises are helpful in fostering flexible thinking:

- Choral speaking of the rows of numbers, i.e., 2, 4, 6... forward and backward;
- Choral speaking of the rows in 2 alternating groups;
- The class is divided into two or more groups and the teacher points to the group who has to say the next number;
- The class recites a row of numbers and when the teacher raises his/her hand, everybody stops and one child has to say the next number;
- These and other drills are done with several children in front of the class; they form a circle and toss a (small and easily handled) ball to each other while reciting the

times tables. The child who throws says the number while throwing, the next child catches the ball and then says the next number while throwing.

Rhythmical reciting is easily learned through the rhythmical memory, while irregular speaking such as in these drills requires more of the head memory to be used. Rhythmic speaking is often done in a semiconscious, dreamlike state, and transition to the work with individual children taking unpredictable turns creates more conscious and wakeful number experiences. This awakening is pedagogically important especially in the math lessons, as opposed to the artistic work such as singing, reciting, or eurythmy where interrupting the flow would be harmful.

Classes who are weak in math usually lack this awakening experience via drills for the head memory and demanding tasks for individual children.

The teacher who utilizes these diverse exercises in his/her teaching will be able to observe how soul forces are called forth: rhythmic movements address the will in connection with the rhythmic system. The body comes to rest when it is only speaking. Drills involving taking unpredictable turns give rise to flexible concept formations. The material (math) becomes a pedagogical tool for calling forth soul forces and awakening the head.

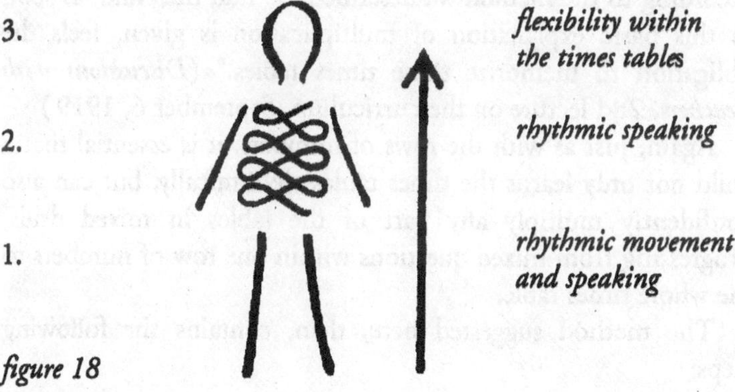

figure 18

When the children have been introduced to multiplication in this manner, stepping exercises are followed by writing down the times tables. For instance, one child walks the row of "x 3" and the class calls out the number of steps, like this:

child	number of steps	class
3	1	3 is 1 x 3
6	2	6 is 2 x 3
9	3	9 is 3 x 3
.	.	.
.	.	.
.	.	.

This drill can only be introduced after the children have learned a) enough numbers through counting exercises, b) the particular row of numbers, and c) multiplication. As soon as these things are known, however, we should not hesitate to energetically teach times tables and drills, taking Rudolf Steiner's advice:

"As soon as the child has begun the change of teeth, one should begin to have it learn the times tables and I would think even the addition table up to maybe 6 or 7. The child should then learn these tables as quickly as possible by rote, after only a basic explanation of what they are, an explanation of multiplication according to the method we described. So that the child, as soon as this basic explanation of multiplication is given, feels the obligation to memorize these times tables." (*Discussions with Teachers*, 2nd lecture on the curriculum, September 6, 1919.)

Again, just as with the rows of numbers, it is essential that a child not only learns the times tables rhythmically, but can also confidently multiply any part of the tables in mixed drills, progressing from mixed questions within one row of numbers to the whole times table.

The method suggested here, then, contains the following steps:

- counting
- rhythmic counting in rows of numbers
- mixed questions within one times table to develop flexibility
- multiplication
- introduction of times tables
- mixed questions within several times tables
- mixed drills among the times tables, including finding the factors for a given product and multiplying the factors to find the product (for the highest degree of flexibility with numbers).

Specific attention should be paid to Steiner's use of the word "obligation" in the above quote. The central pedagogical task after the child enters school is remembering learned information through will. The necessary balance of imaginative forces is represented in the math lessons by math stories, student's and teacher's creativity in the rhythmic exercises, and other ways. Challenging the head memory in math is the necessary counterweight to those parts of the lesson emphasizing imagination.

Planning Arithmetic Main Lesson Blocks for First Grade

Usually we have twelve weeks available for math blocks in first grade. These can easily be divided into three blocks of four weeks each. Since wintertime is especially suitable for mathematics, these blocks might be placed in late fall, in winter, and at Easter. During the last weeks of the school year, the work with numbers will be reviewed. Some teachers prefer to take the number work regularly into the rhythmic part of other Main Lesson blocks.

The way the content of the curriculum is arranged within each block depends very much on the teacher's enthusiasm for mathematics and on the particular constellation of abilities in the class. In general, however, it would be advisable to present in the first block the different aspects in a very relaxed mood. The analytic process in the introduction of numbers and of the four processes is important, as is security in counting, in writing numbers, and in comprehension of small groups of numbers. The numbers should become a movement experience through rhythmic exercises. Simple written arithmetic problems can also be worked out without the symbols for the processes. The teacher should recognize existing weaknesses in computation as early as possible and treat them through rhythmic practice to develop comprehension of numbers.

The second block can raise the characteristics of each of the four processes more clearly into consciousness, name them, and introduce the symbols of the processes. (This is possible if one enters quickly into mathematical activities in the first block and does not lose time with a lengthy and uneconomical introduction of numbers.) Simple addition sequences can be practiced. Working with these sequences prepares the way for multiplication tables. Writing and counting numbers can be extended up to 120.

The third math block continues the work of the previous blocks, but the emphasis is on mastering the first multiplication tables. The children should have a clear understanding of the order of the numbers through their repeated rhythmical counting practice and should feel comfortable with basic computations. Skilled children should not be forced to express numerical relations with counting materials. Children who can calculate freely without the aid of counters need to be acknowledged for this. (See section on Math Materials in the following chapter.)

We plant many seeds in the first school year which come to fruition only in the second year. Therefore, we can observe calmly how the different children gradually develop mathematical skills and make what they have learned their own. In mathematics, as in music, skills vary greatly. What one child learns easily will have to be developed slowly by another. It is very important that children have no fear of failuren. This can lead to serious, sometimes lifelong, handicaps in mathematical ability. If the teacher and students share great enthusiasm in their math activities, many children will be able to do in the second year what they could not yet do in the first year. A minimal formal treatment of the material in the first year is very important for progress in the second year.

The following chapter presents some indications of how to work with children who are slower or who have mathematical learning difficulties.

MATH WEAKNESSES AND DEVELOPMENTAL FOUNDATIONS OF MATH

Math weaknesses are similar to dyslexia in that they are a complex problem with a variety of manifestations. Many questions about math weaknesses are in need of further research. This chapter attempts to contribute to establishing an anthroposophical framework for this research. For the teacher, this information can guide his/her observations and point out easily overlooked problem areas.

There is, as already said, no uniform syndrome named "math disability." Similar behavior patterns of partial or total inability to perform math can have many different causes. Also, several different fields of literature deal with the problem and, coupled with the variety of causes, make a thorough study of the topic difficult.

On the one hand, many studies have been done on low math performance, mostly focusing on mistakes made in calculations. Such errors as choosing the wrong process or the incorrect use of rules (i.e. adding two fractions by adding both numerators and denominators) point out particularly difficult aspects of a given math problem for children. Based on this research, a great number of teaching tips have been proposed and tested. The actual math weakness is generally not covered at all, however.

Other fields of research are covered by the literature in learning psychology, special education, psychiatry, neurophysiology, etc. Special attention deserves to be paid to the psychomotor work of Kiphard et al.

We will now turn to several types of math weaknesses and their causes.

Instructional Causes of Math Weaknesses

a) A specific case of math weakness can be the result of a change in methods. This can always be considered a cause when a child changed schools or teachers. The chances of math difficulty increase when the method used is closely tied to the use of certain materials, for example, Cuisinaire rods of different lengths and colors for different numbers. If the new teacher uses different materials or none at all, the subject may be unrecognizable for the child, and then the performance is low.

b) Related to the above scenario can be a method tied to particular material with a relatively abrupt change to abstract problems. The child feels unable to perform the required tasks without the usual aids and fails. One example for this is the introduction of powers tied to dimensions of line, area, and space. For children who were taught the first three powers in a visual way, the higher ones must remain a mystery because they are completely abstract. The instructional error was to rely on one-sided geometric explanations for arithmetical concepts.

c) One particular case of instructional error was a reform plan for math curricula in Germany in the 60's and 70's. An attempted unified approach based on logic was found to be ineffective and led to specific cases of math disability that had no known constitutional basis. The interesting aspect of this experiment was that there were some students who subconsciously rejected this formal logical approach and fled into math disability, yet when taught in another method based more on developmental appropriateness they were immediately ready and able to learn. We see a glimpse into the fight for human thinking and intelligence in this situation.

d) Switching languages or being forced to learn a new one can contribute to math weakness. Children who were taught math in one language and then have to switch because of a move to another country are affected, and even children who experience only a language change and learn all their math in the new language show difficulty. Even adults who are completely comfortable in another language frequently revert to their mother tongue when calculating, with waiters in ethnic restaurants as a well known example. Math is not a common part of everyday language and thus not as well learned in another language, especially since most math habits hark directly back to elementary school and remain unchanged even in old age unless specific continuation training is taken. We have experienced successful transitions, however, in children who were taught math without math language for a while (i.e., through drawings and through drills in everyday language) and then were able to learn math in the new language without difficulty.

Since Waldorf schools are attended by many children from other countries, this should be noted in the cases where the children are entering a grade higher than the first. Even such minor differences as the names for numbers (for example, twenty-one in English and one-and-twenty in German) can add to math difficulties and can be helpfully brought to the child's attention if the foreign language teacher also does some math in the foreign language lessons.

e) Unfortunately, there is even a Waldorf-specific cause of math weaknesses: remaining in the rhythmic learning too long or too exclusively. As was described above, the rhythmic part of math consists of learning rhythms through stomping, clapping, and so forth. Used exclusively, these can lead to certain difficulties.

Throughout the past few years I have been repeatedly consulted in cases of a partial math disability in otherwise normally capable children. These weaknesses were especially evident in third grade or later. In these cases I first examine the motor development of the child (more about this in a later section) and if there seem to be no weaknesses I begin to ask: "How much is 6 x 7?" and observe the child's reaction very carefully. If the child silently recites the row of 7's, maybe even counts off with the fingers, and stops at 6 x 7 and answers "42," I have found an instructional cause for the child's weakness.

In second or even first grade, about a third of all children discover that one doesn't have to recite all the ... x 7's to know what the solution is. Some teachers take this transition for granted and can feel successful in their method since a third of the class is able to do this without major effort. But a child who is still reciting the entire row of numbers is hopelessly behind from then on. In a few instances, such as multiplying small numbers, it can be successful, but mostly the child learns that s/he is not able to do the work the teacher expects.

In order to overcome the barriers built up by this experience, I ask the child: *"Which multiplication problem can you answer right away?" "None, I can't do them," the child says. "Well, I don't think that's true. Let's find out what you can answer right away. Do you know how much is 1 x 7?" "Yes, of course, it's 7!" "Well, can you tell me any others you know?" "Yes, 10 x 7 is 70."*

Usually the children also know 11 x 7 = 77, 7 x 7 = 49 and 2 x 7 = 14. I then write down a times table and underline all the answers the child can readily give. Then I say, "Now I want you to remember one more answer 35 = 5 x 7 (or 5 x 7 = 35)." The child is thus asked to remember one more product and I make sure that we practice the answer several times along with the other known answers before we write it down. Then the child looks up suddenly and asks (at least this happened to me in several cases) "You mean I can just say it like that?"

The child has suffered from his/her failure because the transition from rhythmic memory to time memory was not guided consciously and appropriately by the teacher.

As discussed in the previous chapters, the teacher has to watch the transition from motor activity to rhythmic speaking to certain individual knowledge very closely. This is a process which has to be lifted from the limbs and the human middle region into the head. The child has to know with absolute and quick certainty that 5 x 7 = 35 without having to think about it first. If this process of head memory formation out of the body is handled successfully, the teacher has the possibility of guiding the relationship between the soul/spirit and the physical body. This in turn results in the refreshing awakeness and certain knowledge that are the signs of a good math lesson.

All of these instructionally caused math weaknesses cause psychological barriers. There are, as yet, no constitutional weaknesses in these children. To overcome these barriers, I recommend finding the causes, working on pedagogical and psychological remedies and strengthening the child through positive comments on his/her effort and work.

Psychological Causes of Math Weaknesses

Aside from the instructionally caused barriers, there are math difficulties with psychological causes usually related to the child's environment. Some children are extremely discouraged because only their mistakes get attention, some are stressed because of their parents' high expectations of them, and some experience fear of failure which can be related to the methods used. These psychological difficulties can lead to a kind of inner cramping or paralysis as soon as math performance is at stake.

I met with one such case several years back. An experienced teacher, who had successfully taught for several years, was asked to solve a math problem during a continuation training course she was taking. Old fears from her own school days returned and paralyzed her to such an extent that she was unable to solve the simplest problems. In the course of a conversation she remembered that she had changed schools in first grade. The resulting traumatic feelings had not been worked out and had resurfaced when she was in a remotely similar position in adulthood.

There are no reliable statistics, but I would venture to guess that more than a quarter of the adult population suffers from some form of math anxiety caused by poor math teaching. Math is the most sensitive subject of all in terms of failure experiences, fear, and blocks which are carried far into adult life. These symptoms are described as arithmaphobia or math phobia and pose a problem during all the years of a student's school life, since, unlike adults, children cannot avoid performance pressures. The only successful treatment I know of is positive evaluations of the child's efforts.

Since high school teachers can still have a positive impact on a student's math performance, I would like to quote a piece of advice the late Georg Hartmann gave to teacher training students in Dornach. "If you are teaching a 9th grade, avoid at all costs giving the class the impression that they know nothing. Instead, show them what they can do." For instance, discuss with them the question of the simplest mathematical problem. Which one is it? Students frequently answer "1 + 1," and when asked for an even simpler one, say "1 x 1 = 1." That one is simpler in that it contains only the number 1, while 1 + 1 = 2 requires one to think of both 1 and 2. Is there an even simpler problem? The students mention 0 x 0 = 0, 0 - 0 = 0, 0 x 1 = 0, and 1 x 0 = 0."

Every math teacher will notice how this question of the simplest mathematical problem can lead into a fruitful discussion about 1 and 0. Whenever I initiated this topic with 9th graders, the students invariably participated enthusiastically. Almost everyone can contribute, and the math lesson benefits in two ways: the teacher can remark positively on the interest and participation of the class, and s/he has created an opportunity to talk about the neutral elements of addition and multiplication—zero and one—which are an important aspect of mathematics.

We cannot discuss the topic in detail, but do want to point out the literature about cases of disabled people, especially epileptics, who sometimes have an astonishing capacity for calculation skills. Also of interest are published studies in the fields of child psychology and psychiatry (see Weinschenk, 1970 or Grissemann and Weber, 1982).

The Origin of Math

As teachers interested in therapeutic insights, we must address above all those math weaknesses that have a constitutional cause. Unfortunately, our schools have neither the staff nor the funding to carry out further research in this area of math disability. Nonetheless we will attempt to create a conceptual framework in this chapter.

The basic question to be asked at the outset of all research and therapeutic work in this field is: What is the basis for mathematical ability? That is related to the even more general question: What is math?

There are several possible approaches to the search for the origin of math. Theoretical mathematicians frequently cite the connection with logic, which defines math as a subspecialty of logic. Others, such as the constructivists, have different interpretations, but they do not seem to explain the development of mathematical thinking in children.

However, in the field of psychology, Jean Piaget explored the developmental aspects of mathematical thinking, and his research was used as the basis for math teaching. These attempts were not very successful, and Piaget himself did not approve of them. He differentiated developmental stages in children's thinking, but was not able to transform his understanding of what math is into a usable math curriculum or method. I emphasize this in view of the fact that many countries' elementary school math programs are supposedly based on Piaget's work. The valuable aspect of his work is the connection between forming the concept of numbers and inner experience of processes.

In his book *The Working Brain*, the neurophysiologist Luria describes the connection between body orientation and math ability. To his surprise, victims of brain damage lost both simultaneously. These kinds of physiological connections are more clearly understood in the light of Steiner's concepts of the twelve senses.

Taken together, the whole spectrum of neurophysiological, psychological, and logical explanations for the nature and origin of mathematics and their correlation with human physiology become very interesting when combined with Steiner's indications for these questions. This combination enables us to develop both an appropriate math curriculum and a therapeutic framework for various cases of math disability.

The anthroposophical approach to math development is based on the following thesis: human math abilities originate in the inner activity of the sense of movement.

An explanation of this follows: When I taught in a 6th grade in Munich, I once drew two lines on the blackboard and asked: "Do these two lines meet?" (figure 19) A very outgoing sanguine boy raised his hand and said, "No." As a recent graduate in math, I was extremely surprised to hear a child say no to this problem. The next boy, however, also said no. What was I to do? I turned to the class and asked, "Who thinks that the lines meet?" A girl raised her hand and said, much to my relief, "Of course they meet." The first boy loudly asked, "But where?" The girl pointed to a spot next to the blackboard. The boy laughed and said, "Go ahead and draw that!"

(Another interesting anecdote involved the same class in 10th grade. In a discussion of the infinite in projective geometry, the same girl again led the class in the right direction to find the answer.)

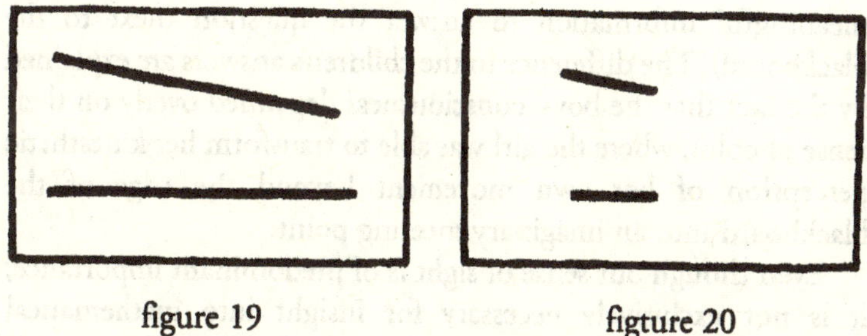

figure 19 figture 20

Let's examine the problem of whether the lines meet. In what way were the boys right when they claimed that the lines did not meet, and in what way was the girl right when she said they did? Let's look at the whole process in detail. When looking at the blackboard, we see colored areas, gray-black for the blackboard and white for the chalk lines. The small white lines prompt us to move along them with our eyes. This eye movement is controlled by our senses of balance and of our own movement. The sense of balance also relates this movement to our body. I suspect that a disturbance or weakening of the sense of balance would make it impossible to determine the point where the two lines meet outside of the blackboard. The girl was able to find this meeting point by continuing the movement suggested by the chalk lines and becoming independent of the color impression of the blackboard.

Even when only two very short lines are given (figure 20), the meeting point can be determined. The sense of color enables us to distinguish the color qualities, and at the transition we are stimulated to move. This movement is controlled by our sense of our own movement (kinesthetic sense), and our sense of balance relates it to our own body position. The perception of our kinesthetic sense is not directed at the color differences any more, but at my own pupil activity. The mathematical perception is not outside, but inside our own bodies. And this is the reason we are able to perceive even where our sense of color no longer supplies meaningful information to answer the question (next to the blackboard). The difference in the children's answers are explained by the fact that the boys' consciousness depended overly on their sense of color, where the girl was able to transform her kinesthetic perception of her own movement beyond the edge of the blackboard into an imaginary meeting point.

Even though our sense of sight is of predominant importance, it is not exclusively necessary for insight into mathematical qualities. Whoever wants to perceive a concrete spatial geometric concept has to be stimulated to experience movement. The specifics of how this is done are relatively unimportant. For instance, I once taught a blind girl in high school and she was able to imagine and draw all geometric figures (line, circle, ellipse, hyperbole, intersections, etc.) when a friend drew the shapes into her hand. Her sense of touch was able to supply the movement experience when the lines were drawn into her hand in chronological sequence.

Our kinesthetic sense (of our own movement) therefore needs one or more senses which perceive the outside world in order for us to perceive and create mathematical concepts. Usually our eye functions like two or even three senses in this regard since it perceives color and executes finely controlled movements. When we think of movement muscles, the first ones to come to mind are legs and arms, but jaw and eye muscles belong in this category, too. Through leg movement we proceed through three dimensional space (propelled by our will), arm movements let us grasp our surrounding space, and eye movement allows us to perceive space through rotation, crossing of vision axes, and accommodation.

The developmental origin of math occurs at the point where the outer movement continues inwardly. The two 6th grade boys who didn't imagine the two lines intersecting outside the blackboard were sanguines and especially gifted physically. However, at that time, they were not yet able to rise above the impressions from outside and to create independent inner movements. This was a combination of a strong reliance on their sense of vision and a reluctance to calm their body sufficiently to imagine various inner movements. The determination of where the two lines intersect is an especially clear challenge to imagine movement beyond that which is given. All mathematical activity has to be able to imagine inner movement even when no outer movement or relations in space are shown.

Actually, a line drawn with chalk on a blackboard is not a line in the mathematical sense, either. So what is the content of geometry? What weaves these geometric figures together? Our inner movements are guided by rays of will and set in motion by our sense of balance, while the physically incarnated ego is in overall charge. Only this ego activity enables me to consciously relate body and environment, inwardly picture the forces at work, and then penetrate them with my thinking. If the sense of balance is upset, the ego is pushed out of the body. In the old days, people used to say that the sky was falling when their sense of balance was not functioning properly. In such a situation mathematical activity is impossible.

In this discussion of the origins of math we have primarily been talking about geometry. How do we became conscious of numbers then? In forming concepts of numbers, judgment plays a different role than it does in geometry. For instance, if I say, "There are three people," the process includes both the inclusion and the exclusion of something. I first form a unit of the objects I have chosen to count, which is the first step in number concept formation. Our "sense of life" (see Rudolf Steiner, *The Foundation of Human Experience,* Lecture 8; also published as *Study of Man*) is involved in this, even though a unit can only be formed mentally if I have both the concept of a unit and the ability to correctly judge what one is. The concept can be used for physical things or for abstract ideas (i.e., for all the trees I see in my garden or for all the prime numbers between 1 and 100).

The determination of any numbers requires this concept of unit and it determines which number we find as an answer. If I ask how many people are in a room, the answer will be different from what it will be if I ask how many men there are or how many chairs there are. The room we are in does not in itself contain a certain amount of things but lets us determine a number relative to the concept of a unit. When we have formed the concept of this particular amount of objects, we can individualize it: How is the unit anchored in a perception or in other concepts?

In other words, when I say to a group of people, "You are seven," I create a context of space and concept by using "you." This unit comes from my thinking. When I look at the objects in my unit with the concept of "people," my concept becomes individualized into every single person. In every case where a concept is anchored in a perception, there is an individualization of the concept. In paying attention to the perception I simultaneously engage in a motor activity in time. If I want to determine the number and not the individuals in this particular group, I have to individualize my concept of people, but turn not to its result but to the process of grasping the concept.

To illustrate this difference, let's imagine a person looking through a telescope while we watch. We cannot know what the person is seeing, but we can observe the motions of his arms and of the telescope. From this observation, we can determine that he has looked at three different objects, but we would not know that they were three ocean liners. We perceive the ships visually, but we are only able to perceive the number of ships by means of our own physical experience of movement.

We therefore experience mathematics in our own activity. The stimulating aspect of math is this experience of world order in our most inward activity. We all know how subjective judgments based on taste or smell can be. When somebody says, "Herring tastes awful", this seems to be an objective statement. Actually, the speaker only commented on his own relationship to herring. However, when somebody says there are 3 herrings on the plate, the dominating truth is the number 3, regardless of our likes or ideologies. If we have judged correctly, there is no conflict.

We have discussed the origin of math so thoroughly because rational therapy and diagnosis of math weaknesses are not possible without this knowledge. Whoever says that math is abstracted perception does not understand it and will not be able to treat math disability successfully. Again, any therapeutic work will have to take into consideration these inner processes taking place during mathematical activity in both children and adults. The interplay between senses perceiving the outside world (sense of touch, sense of color) and those perceiving the body (sense of balance, kinesthetic sense) is of particular importance in this work.

Constitutional Cause of Math Weaknesses

It is important to understand the physical basis of math development in order to identify snags and the constitutional weaknesses they may signal. To determine constitutional readiness for math in a child we offer the following 3 steps:

Step 1: We begin by assessing the development and maturity of the child's senses. Some senses are relatively well developed at birth (smell, taste) while others form gradually (sense of balance, kinesthetic sense).

Observation of physical ability also plays an important role in math ability assessment. We begin by observing large and small motor skills. How does the child walk? How does the child set its feet down? How do the arms move while walking?

In curative homes, often one can distinguish healthy children from even slightly handicapped ones by their walk alone—any disturbance of harmonious muscle interplay is immediately noticeable. Even slight soul imbalances impact the maturation of movement.

We can assess a child's coordination very easily by asking him/her to remove one shoe. Children with imbalances like to sit down to do this. When asked to do it standing up, they try to lean on a wall or other object. (They have lots of practice in compensating for their weakness.) If we insist on having the child remove the shoe while standing up, it is possible that the child falls over when lifting a foot. What is noticeable is that these children attempt to lift a foot without compensatory movements for balance.

When we lift our leg we are not just moving the leg muscles but coordinating our whole body; our neck, chest and back, belly and feet are all active. Learning how to walk means we can not only put one foot in front of the other but also harmoniously coordinate the movement of our entire body. This unified physical harmony is a prerequisite for math ability and every child should be observed for signs of this movement body falling apart.

Another essential aspect of physical readiness can be assessed in the next exercise: we ask the child to climb onto a chair and observe the motions of the upper body. Are the arms actively supporting the climbing act or are they disconnected? How is the head held? What are the fingers doing? What is the expression on the child's face? Imbalanced children frequently move in ways that are unrelated to the intended movement. Small unintended motions however, such as sticking out the tongue in concentration, are probably harmless.

Another aspect of math ability testing is body orientation. In the rhythmic part of the Waldorf school main lesson we practice this important skill with exercises like this: *"Put your right index finger to your left ear, your left pinkie to your nose,"* and so on. Thus some everyday parts of the lesson have therapeutic value. Laterality or handedness also belongs to the assessment. There is a wealth of literature relating laterality to dyslexia or math disability and motor development in general. While we cannot discuss this topic in detail, we would like to mention that there has also been some anthroposophical research, mostly regarding the role of the ego in taking up the physical body, and the etheric forces being freed after the change of teeth.

Motor disturbances can also be observed in children who are raised in an intellectual environment. One could even say certain parents predispose their children to this. Usually the observable effects are tense or even cramped movements, nervous "running into things," and so on. These sometimes result in fixations on certain numbers or even an exceptional talent for math. Where some children seem unable to find the healthy physical foundation required for math, these intellectualized children seem to fixate early on the inner concepts of space and time. Also related to this is the observation that adult mathematicians frequently move in awkward and uncoordinated ways. I suspect that this is related to an emphasis on the conceptual as opposed to the perceptual. The students also assert that they are able to recognize mathematicians from a distance because they are pale, take flat steps, walk with their eyes lowered and are unusually quiet. This anecdotal evidence, even if true, should not be taken as a counter argument to our basic tenet that math ability requires a healthy physical foundation. We think it points out the need for a further step in assessment.

Step 2: When ready to enter school, a child has reached a developmental step where the part of the ether body connected to the nervous system is partially freed from the organic processes to be used by the soul for mental imaging and memory. This step, also called the birth of the ether body or of intelligence, is not yet the beginning of causal thinking, which happens in pre-puberty. The task of teaching consists now in making sure that the children can grasp the liberated etheric forces with their will, with their ego. Piaget's studies show the obvious difference in thinking at this developmental level. His level of "concrete operations" points out how independent of sense perception the life of mental images has now become. The child can picture processes in reverse that are not physically reversible, and can think through different solutions to a problem. If the ego cannot take hold properly of the mental and memory forces at this age, there is the danger that "associative thinking" will result, a thinking where one image follows the next without logical connection and without guidance from the ego or will. To practice the orderly permeation of imagination by the will forces, we use times table drills.

Piaget's "concrete operations" is another term for the inner experience of space and movement and their sense processes. The school age child is also ready to freely "compose" with sense perceptions. A future cook has to be able to combine taste and smell impressions, a painter colors, a musician sounds. In order to successfully calculate in math, inner experiences of space and movement have to be created. It is not enough to reproduce those that are outside; they must be actively created within.

In order to take the first step (physical readiness) and this second step (imaging free of sense perception) into our therapeutic assessment, we always begin with physical activity and end with quiet sitting while inwardly creating movement and number concepts. This is the beginning of an approach based on knowledge of the human being.

There is an important step in between sense perception and imagination of movement: touching one's own body. For instance, if we draw a number on the child's back, the child can perceive the touch, but has to accompany this touch with inner movement in order to recognize which number is being drawn, since s/he cannot immediately physically imitate the movement of somebody else's hand drawing on the back. It would be interesting to study whether feeling the drawing on the back is accompanied by tiny movements of the eye muscles.

A similar process of inner movement has to accompany the task of guessing how many fingers are being held. An extreme case of math disability drove this home to me when I interviewed a fifteen-year-old girl in 6th grade whose math performance was at 1st grade level. What was the problem? I asked the girl to put her hand on the table, covered three fingers, and asked her, how many fingers are covered?" She looked at me in complete surprise and said, "I don't know." I uncovered her hand and she counted the fingers with her other hand "1, 2, 3. Three fingers." I then covered up two fingers and asked again how many I was covering. Again she didn't know and had to count them from the outside like unrelated objects. In order to try to imagine how this girl felt her body from the inside, I thought of her hands as completely wrapped up in cloths. Interestingly, sometimes the drawings of children with this "finger agnosia" reflect their state.

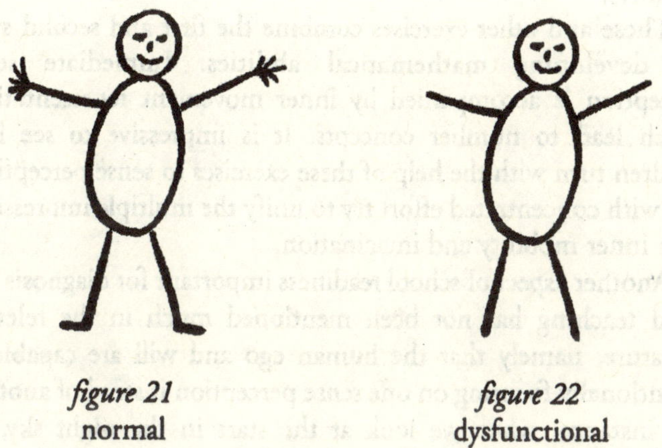

figure 21
normal

figure 22
dysfunctional

The simple version of the finger test consists of asking the names of the fingers and then asking the child to move one particular finger ("Wiggle your left ring finger!"). This perception of fingers and toes can be practiced early on by playing finger guessing games. It is really quite amazing to teach the child awareness for body periphery by going from the one bone in the upper arm to the two bones in the lower arm to the many bones in the wrist and fingers. In the book by Kranich et al. on form drawing 1992, Kranich's article gives more detailed explanations about the importance of feeling one's own body as a prerequisite for math ability.

Another useful game for strengthening number concept formation is "number guessing." Each child has his/her unique sense structure and takes in different perceptions from those of the next child, just as a chestnut tree takes different nutrients out of the earth than an oak tree does. Optically dominant children experience the world differently from acoustically oriented ones, and since we have to initiate number formation via an outer sense, we have opportunities for offering optical, acoustical, tactile experiences, or experiences of warmth and taste for determining numbers.

These and other exercises combine the first and second steps for developing mathematical abilities. Immediate sense perception is accompanied by inner movement representations which lead to number concepts. It is impressive to see how children turn with the help of these exercises to sense perceptions and with concentrated effort try to unify the multiple impressions with inner mobility and imagination.

Another aspect of school readiness important for diagnosis and good teaching has not been mentioned much in the relevant literature, namely that the human ego and will are capable of intentionally focusing on one sense perception instead of another. For instance, when we look at the stars in the night sky, we perceive light and color. Unconsciously, we also perceive the star's position in space in relation to our own, by seeing it "in the upper right, in front." When our ego is truly in control of our senses, we are able to intentionally switch from the perception of light and color to the perception of position in space. Where the boys who said the lines did not intersect were not yet able to free themselves from the color perception, the girl who said they met on the wall had more of the necessary flexibility and control. This skill of separating sense perceptions from one another is usually not achieved before the 12th year of life. The laws of congruence in elementary geometry require that the child be able to grasp form independent of position in space. If the children are not yet able to master this, teaching this subject should obviously be postponed. My chapter on geometry in the Kranich et al. book on form drawing explains this in more detail.

Step 3: When the child is showing both healthy physical maturity and the ability to coordinate inner movement, space, and number concepts, the third step consists of recognizing relationships between objects through conceptual thinking. This is the beginning of actual math, which defines and describes specific figures, determines their relationship, formulates general rules and relates them logically to each other. This topic does not need to be elaborated here since this third step is the content of all math education at all levels of schooling.

We have now described the three main steps of the development of math ability:

- physical senses and their coordination (body)
- inner senses and imagination (soul)
- recognition of objective rules (mind, spirit).

Math disabilities can be traced back to snags in any one of the three steps. This conceptual framework enables us to diagnose different causes and design therapeutic measures for disabilities. Below is a summary of the essential observations and tests necessary for diagnosis. We are assuming that low math performance has already been found and that instructional or psychological causes have been ruled out.

Step 1: physical development

- large and small muscle movement
- coordination: any associative movements?
- body awareness, especially fingers
- laterality (crossed dominance etc.)
- spasms or other anomalies

Step 2: perception and imagination (depending on the age of the child, variations in abilities are normal)

- Can figures be recognized as similar in different positions?
- Are number concepts independent of outer objects?
- Are numbers used independently of visual images or other (even imaginary) sense perceptions?
- Are any two senses too closely connected?
- In short, we are testing the child's inner mobility in using forms and numbers.

Step 3: transition to relationships between numbers

- Where is the child unable to perform the necessary inner activity?
- Where is the imagination too closely tied to the senses?

Both the physical and the soul mobility assessment facilitate insight into remedial action requirements, with special attention to coordination and intentional separation of the senses. If the child's development has generally been healthy and if the therapy has been able to bring order to the required soul activities, then the mental work necessary for grasping math concepts can usually proceed unimpeded.

Math Materials

In conclusion I would like to discuss one particular aspect of the use of math materials. Especially in curative education we frequently observe teachers using a very sense oriented and materialistic approach in trying to reach the children. Even more than the regular math curriculum with its logic blocks, Cuisinaire rods, and other materials, special education has always used methods based on tactile and visual sense impression. We would like to contrast these techniques with another approach described in Steiner's lecture cycle *Universe, Earth and Man* (2nd lecture) where he associates math teaching with the human healing forces:

In ancient times, this raising oneself up to the spirit was a healing element and it would be beneficial for humanity to understand this once again. Then it would be able to understand the great mission of the anthroposophical movement as well. What else is this mission, after all, but to lift human beings into spiritual worlds so that they can once again look into the worlds they descended from! There will be no somnambulistic sleep imposed on humankind in the future and self-consciousness will remain awake and aware. A strong spiritual force will become active in human nature. Then wisdom and insight into the higher worlds will once again be restoring and healing for human nature. Today this connection between spirit and healing is so well hidden that people uninitiated into mystery wisdom do not know much about it since they are unable to observe the subtle circumstances in question. But those who are able to look more deeply into it know that healing can depend on deeply hidden criteria.

Let's take the case of a person, for instance, who catches a certain disease, a disease with inner causes, not a broken thigh or an upset stomach, since those have outer causes. Everyone who wants to truly learn about these things will soon realize that the possibility of healing is much greater in a person who enjoys math activities than in somebody who dislikes math. This fact points out the remarkable connection between a person's mental/spiritual life and the conditions for his/her outer health.

Of course, it isn't as though mathematical thinking healed people. We have to define this more exactly: different healing conditions are necessary for someone who can assimilate mathematical concepts than for a someone who hasn't done this. Suppose two people have an identical disease. This doesn't happen in reality, but let's use this hypothetical example. The first one wants absolutely nothing to do with mathematical concepts, the other lives for them. It could happen that it's impossible to cure the non-mathematician, where the other case responds to appropriate measures. This is a very real possibility.

As another example, there are totally different health conditions in two people, one of whom is an atheist in the worst way and the other one is devoutly religious. Again it could happen that you use the same medications for both and the religious one recovers and the other doesn't. These are correlations that for most people today seem almost absurd, and yet it is so.

Why is this? It is based on the fact that sense-filled concepts have a totally different influence on human nature than sense-free ones. Imagine the difference between a person who loves math and one who hates it. The second one says, "I should think about all that? I only want what I can experience through my senses." It is very useful for the human inner life to live in concepts that cannot be seen, and it is just as useful to live with religious concepts because these also refer to things that cannot be grasped with our hands, that do not refer to material reality and are, in short, sense-free. These are all facts that will be of great influence for teaching principles once people consider the spiritual realm important.

Let's take the simple concept that 3 x 3 = 9, for instance. Children best learn this concept when it is taught sense-free. It is detrimental to have them lay down 3 x 3 beans for too long since they will not free themselves of the sense impression. But when you get the children used to counting with the fingers first, but not for too long, and follow this with pure mathematical thinking, then this will be a healthy and orderly process for the children. We see how little understanding of this there is in our time when the exact opposite process happens in education. Aren't our schools now using counting machines, where addition, subtraction, etc. are shown to the eye through various balls? What should be grasped only by the mind is here made, as they say, clear to the senses.

This may be convenient, but those who think this is pedagogical know nothing of the deeper curative pedagogy rooted in the force of the spirit. A person who has from childhood on been exposed to sense-based concepts will be more difficult to heal, because his nervous system is living under unhealthy conditions, than someone who has known sense-free concepts throughout his/her life. The more people get used to thinking in ways that are independent of physical things, the easier they will be to heal. This is the reason traditional medicine gave people symbols such as triangles, figures, or combinations of numbers. Their function, beyond their other usefulness, was to raise people above that which can be seen with the naked eye. If I put a triangle in front of myself and look at it, it has no great value. But if I grasp that it is a symbol of the higher trinity of man, it is a healing concept for the spirit.

These words can give food for thought to anyone teaching out of anthroposophical developmental principles. Shouldn't we try to teach even the children who have difficulties along this three-step path, beginning with body-sense exercises, moving on to inner sense activity and concepts based on imagination, and arriving at the purely mental content without outside perceptions?

The deepest pedagogical challenge for math is education toward the spirit. Unlike any other subject, it can give young people the certainty that through their innermost activity they can gain an objective truth about the world that is not based on passive perceptions, such as color or sound. The content of this truth is clearly delineated and is a universal tool for understanding the outer world. What we have reaped from our inner activity connects us with objective truth about the world.

The anthroposophical mathematician Louis Locher-Ernst called math the "preschool for realization of the spirit." We who are striving to support and heal the weak constitutions of children should never lose sight of this great truth: that the spirit shines forth brilliantly in earthly existence!

APPENDIX I

A Play about Numbers
by Ernst Bühler, Switzerland

The children line up and count.

Class: We are the first grade and play the number game.

Catherine: I am the One. I am the whole. Everything is contained within me. I am round and beautiful.

Thomas and Harold: We are the Two. We are more than you. We are two friends.

Class: Yes, you are two friends but only one pair.

Iris, Matthew, Benjamin: We are the Three. We are more than you. We are father, mother, and child.

Class: Yes, you are three, but only one family.

Anne, Florian, Sonia, Rolja: We are the four winds. We are more than you.

Red: I am the North wind.

Blue: I am the East wind.

Green: I am the South wind.

Yellow: I am the West wind.

Class: Yes, you are four winds, but you are only one air.

Michelle, Ethel, Lucia, Yasmine, Judith: We are the rose. We are more than you: 1 2 3 4 5. We have five petals.

Class: Yes, you are five petals, but just one rose.

Christopher, Fred, Kevin, Matt, Marcus, Daniel: We are the six sides of the crystal. We are more than you: 1 2 3 4 5 6.

Class: Yes, you are six sides of the crystal, but only one crystal.

Carmen, Nicole, Raphael, Jessica, Larisaa, Birgit, Reagan:
We are the seven days of the week. We are more than you: Monday, Tuesday, Wednesday, Thursday, Friday, Saturday, Sunday.
Old Monday often shakes his head,
he'd like to spend his days in bed.
But Tuesday is heroic strong,
her mighty arms can do no wrong.
Wednesday arrives, his feet are fleet
'Let's dance,' says he, 'get off your seats.'
Thursday has time to listen well
when each child has a verse to tell.
Friday ties wedding wreaths so wide
they fit the bridegroom and the bride.
On Saturday we wash and mend
because the week is at its end.
Sunday everyone likes the best
she wears the golden crown of rest.

Class: Yes, you are seven days, but only one week.

Patrick: I am the zero, a magical woman. Whoever I touch is changed forever: 10 20 30 40 50 60 70.

Class: Dear guests, we thank you for your time
you listened to our number play.
You might have missed the 8 and 9,
we'll save those for another day.
We'll show you now how we can count
in 2's and 3's and up and down.
2 4 6 8 10 12 14 16 18 20
3 6 9 12 15 18 21 24 27 30.

A Math Play for the 1st Grade
by Ernst Schuberth, Germany

The class walks in and lines up, counting all the while.

We are the children of grade one, we know our math quite well;
we count together or one by one, as clearly as a bell.

(Some of the children, i.e. 6, 12, or 24, form a circle while the rest of the class recites with them.)

In the beginning, all the world was One.
This was before the work that God has done.

(The children hold hands and walk around in a circle.)

But when God thought of making night and day,
then there were Two, and One was then away.

(The children form two circles.)

When man saw God, himself, and nature, too,
the three was born, and yet still all was one.
Wildflowers bloomed and happy cows said "moo."
God said, "The three's the best thing I have done."

(The two circles rearrange themselves into a three-petaled flower shape. Then all the children form a line again and turn to the audience.)

Thus were the first three numbers made,
you'll now see 4, 5, 6, 7, 8.

(The children now show the numbers 5 - 8 with their bodies. For some, two children pose one behind the other to form the number with their arms and legs while the teacher counts out the numbers.)

That is not all we 1st graders know,
we can also say numbers in a row.

(The teacher begins with a number and the children stomp around the circle in rhythm, i.e. 1, 2, 1, 2... or 1, 2, 3, 1, 2, 3, ...The bold numbers are emphasized. A tambourine or triangle can help the children keep their rhythm.)

The numbers continue, go on and on,
we like to say them both up and down.

(The children count from 1 to 20, forward and backward, loudly or quietly, at the teacher's direction. There can also be variations between groups and single children.)

And if you are thinking "This class is not bad!",
just wait till we show you how well we can add!

(Five children step forward and form a pentagon.)

It's really amazing what we five can do
by counting, combining, and adding up, too.

(The five children form different groups and the class says aloud what the teacher points to, i.e. 2 + 1 + 2 .)

5 = 2 + 1 + 2
5 = 4 + 1
5 = 3 + 1 + 1
5 = 1 + 2 + 2
5 = ...
You see, the five can be so many things.
we even saw it do Olympic rings!
We're leaving now. . .

(The children form a line and stomp in rhythm while walking out.)

2 4 6 8 10 12 14 16 18 20 22 24

(The children come back walking backwards.)

24 22 20 18 16 14 12 10 8 6 4 2

. . . and coming back!
We thought, this row of 2 is easy now,
we'll just come back and take a bow,
then walk back out again, you'll see,
and stomp the row of 2 and row of 3.

*(The class walks out stomping 1,2, 1,2,3, 1,2, 1,2,3, 1,2,....
The 1,2 can also be stepped backwards.)*

APPENDIX 2

Rudolf Steiner on the Introduction of Processes in Connection with the Temperaments

Rudolf Steiner speaks about introducing the four processes in relationship to the temperaments, in Discussions with Teachers, *1919, 4th lecture (British edition):*

Let us start from addition, and first see what our conception of addition should be. Let us suppose that I have some beans or a heap of elderberries. For our present task I will take it for granted that the children can count, which indeed they must learn to do first of all. A child counts them and finds he has 27. 'Yes' I say '27, that is the sum.' We proceed from the sum, not from the addenda. You can follow the psychological significance of this in my theory of knowledge. (See Rudolf Steiner: A Theory of Knowledge Implicit in Goethe's World Conception) We must now divide the whole into the addenda, into parts or into little heaps. We will have one heap of elderberries, let us say 12, another heap, let us say 7, yet another, let us say 3, and one more, let us say 5; this will represent the whole number of our elderberries:

$$27 = 12 + 7 + 3 + 5\,.$$

We work out our arithmetical process from the sum total 27. I should let this process be done by a number of children with a pronounced phlegmatic temperament. You will gradually come to realize that this kind of addition is specially suitable for the phlegmatics. Then, as the process can be reversed, I should call up some choleric children, and gather the elderberries together again, but arranging them so that 5 and 3 and 7 and 12 make up the 27. In this way the choleric child does the reverse process. But addition in itself is the arithmetical rule that is particularly suitable for phlegmatic children.

Now I choose out one of the melancholic children. I say: 'Here is a little heap of elderberries. Count them for me.' He discovers that there are, let us say, 8 in the heap. 'Now', I say, 'I don't want 8, I only want 3. How many elderberries must you take away to leave me only 3?' He will discover that 5 must be taken away. Subtraction in this form is the one of the four rules that is particularly suited to melancholic children. Now I call up a sanguine child and let him do the reverse process. I ask him what has been taken away and I let him tell me that if I take away 5 from 8, I shall have 3 left. Thus the sanguine child is to carry out the reverse arithmetical process. I would only like to add that in general it is the melancholic children who have a special connection with subtraction carried out as I have described.

Now I take a child from the sanguine group. Again I put down a heap of elderberries, but I must take care that the numbers fit. I must arrange it beforehand, otherwise we shall find ourselves involved in fractions. I let the child count out 56 elderberries. 'Now look, here I have 8 elderberries and now you must tell me how often you find 8 elderberries contained in 56.' So you see that multiplication leads to a dividing up. The child finds that the answer is 7. Now let the sum be done in the reverse way by a melancholic child and say: 'But this time I do not want to discover how often the 8 is contained in the 56, but what is the number that is contained 7 times in 56.' I always let the reverse process be carried out by the opposite temperament.

Next I introduce the choleric to division—from the smaller number to the greater—by saying: 'Look, here you have a little pile of 8; I want to know from you in which number you can find 8 seven times.' And he must find the answer: 'In 56, in a pile of 56.' Then I let the phlegmatic children work out the opposite process, ordinary division. The former is the way in which I use division for the choleric child, for in this form division is preeminently the rule of Arithmetic that belongs to the choleric children.

By keeping on constantly in this way I find it possible to make use of the four rules of Arithmetic to arouse the interest of the four temperaments. Adding is related to the phlegmatic temperament, subtracting to the melancholic, multiplying to the sanguine, and dividing, working back to the dividend, to the choleric. This is what I beg you to consider, following on to what N. has been telling us.

It is very important not to go on working in a monotonous way, doing nothing but adding for six months and then subtracting and so on, but where possible to take all four arithmetical rules fairly quickly one after another, and then to practice them all, but at first only up to about the number 40. So we shall not teach Arithmetic as is laid down in an ordinary curriculum, but by practicing them, these four rules can be assimilated almost simultaneously. You will find that this will save you a great deal of time, and in this way the children can work one rule in with another. For division is connected with subtraction, and multiplication is really only a repetition of addition. So you can even change things about and give subtraction, for example, to the choleric child.

BIBLIOGRAPHY

Grissemann, H. and A. Weber. *Diagnose und Behandlung der Sprach- und Lesestörungen* (Specific Math Weaknesses: Diagnosis and Therapy). Bern: Verlag Hans Huber, 1982.

Kranich, E.-M. *Mathematische Früherziehung im Vorschulalter als psychologisch-pädagogisches Problem* (Early Math Education in Preschools: A Psychological-Pedagogical Problem). In *Der schweizerische Kindergarten,* 3/1970.

——. Mathematik im Vorschulalter (Math in Preschool). In *Erziehungskunst,* Stuttgart 2/1975.

Kranich, E.-M. et al. *Formenzeichnen: Die Entwicklung des Formensinns in der Erziehung* (Form Drawing: The Development of the Sense of Form in Education). Stuttgart: Verlag Freies Geistesleben, 1992.

Locher-Ernst, L. *Mathematik als Vorschule zur Geisterkenntnis (Mathematics as a Path to Spiritual Insight).* Dornach, 1984.

Luria, A.R. *The Working Brain: An Introduction to Neuropsychology.* London: Allen Lane, 1973.

Maturana, H.R. and E. J.Varela., *The Tree of Knowledge: The Biological Roots of Human Understanding.* Boston: New Science Library, 1987.

Piaget, J. *Psychology of Intelligence.* London: Routledge and Paul, 1950.

Schuberth, E. *Die Modernisierung des mathematischen Unterrichts (Modernizing Math Education).* Stuttgart, 1991.

——. *Erziehung in einer Computergesellschaft (Education in a Computer Society).* Stuttgart, 1990.

——. Geometrische und menschenjundliche Grundlagen für das

Formenzeichnen (Foundations of Form Drawing: Geometry and Knowledge of the Human Being). In E. M. Kranich et al., *Formenzeichnen. Die Entwicklung des Formenzeichnen in der Erziehung*. Stuttgart, 1992.

Steiner, Rudolf. *Discussions with Teachers.* Hudson, New York: Anthroposophic Press, 1997. This edition includes the three lectures on the curriculum given September 6, 1919. (GA 295)

——. *The Education of the Child and Early Lectures on Education.* Hudson, New York: Anthroposophic Press, 1996. (GA 34)

——. *The Foundation of Human Experience.* Hudson, New York: Anthroposophic Press, 1996. Also published as *Study of Man.* (GA 293)

——. *The Kingdom of Childhood.* Hudson, New York: Anthroposophic Press, 1995. (GA 311)

——. *Practical Advice to Teachers.* London: Rudolf Steiner Press, 1976. (GA 295)

——. *The Science of Knowing.* Spring Valley, New York: Mercury, 1996. Formerly published as *A Theory of Knowledge Implicit in Goethe's World Conception.* (GA 3)

——. *Truth and Knowledge.* Blauvelt, New York: Steinerbooks, 1981. (GA 2)

——. *Universe, Earth and Man.* London: Rudolf Steiner Press, 1987. (GA 105)

——. *World History and the Mysteries in the Light of Anthroposophy.* London: Rudolf Steiner Press, 1997. Formerly published as *World History in the Light of Anthroposophy.* (GA 233)

Weinschenk, C. *Rechenstörungen: Ihre Diagnostik und Therapie (Arithmetic Dysfunctions: Their Diagnosis and Therapy).* Bern, 1970.